BULL!

144 STUPID STATEMENTS FROM THE MARKET'S FALLEN PROPHETS

Greg Eckler and L. M. Mac Donald

**Andrews McMeel
Publishing**

Kansas City

BULL!

03 04 05 06 07 VAI 10 9 8 7 6 5 4 3 2 1

ISBN: 0-7407-3612-4

Library of Congress Catalog Card Number: 2002043875

ATTENTION: SCHOOLS AND BUSINESSES

INTRODUCTION

The people profiled in this book crawled out of a wide variety of holes to enter the public consciousness. Wall Street, Washington, and Media are all represented with distinction. And why not? In the 1990s businesspeople went from being shunned to being feted as celebrities and cult heroes. The New Economy man literally shrugged off his "suit" role by adopting a more relaxed, creative approach to business life. The "stodgy" old economy, the one where you make something, charge for it, and come up with a profit, suddenly seemed hopelessly outdated. Financial shows, once drab and shunted to the back of the news, started to look like *Entertainment Tonight*, with breathless reporters in tony black glasses. Financial reporters got their own shows, which in turn got their own cable networks. And as any network exec can tell you, networks need stars. Suddenly average Americans, if there were any left, couldn't escape the CEOs, analysts, reporters, and politicians telling them to buy, buy, buy. They begged us to borrow, pleaded with us to stay in the market, scared us out of selling, reassured us that we'd reached bottom while CEOs and their ilk were selling everything except what they got paid to sell. And on it goes. These same people continue to reassure us. They aren't cult heroes. They're cult leaders. *Come on . . . just sip the Kool-Aid . . .*

Morons. Tools. Jerkwads. Feel free to use any of these words when glimpsing the gorgeous stupidity of the big shots on display in these pages. These are the people who supposedly knew more than the rest of us, when they clearly knew the least. While our stock market was heading down the path of ruin, they were tripping over each other to say, "This is a great idea and I want some credit!" Okay, some of them weren't dumb. They were thieving liars. We may never know for sure which ones were honest and which were con men, which ones were buying snake oil and which were selling it, but don't be discouraged. Even though many of these knobs made off with our millions, they're now forced to spend the vast majority of it on security.

Sure, more than half of us foolishly threw money down the stock market drain. Maybe we were caught up in "infectious greed," a phrase recently popularized by perhaps the greatest hero of the stock market bubble, a man so mythologized in his genius that nobody is yet ready to accept that he was as entranced by the New Economy crap as anyone else. A man who, given all the tools of the Federal Reserve to keep our economy in equilibrium, decided to spend the bulk of his time coining phrases.

The qualification for inclusion in this rogues' gallery isn't being wrong but rather being unquestionably and unforgivably stupid (being wrong tended to follow that almost every time, if not immediately). Yes, people, even professionals, make mistakes. Sometimes a weatherman calls for sun and it turns out to be rainy. But these mistakes aren't like that. These are like a weatherman calling for sun and it turns out to be the hurricane of the century. And if he's been a weatherman for twenty years and written five books on weather forecasting and charges $30,000 for a speech on meteorology and can't detect the hurricane of the century . . . well, maybe somebody needs to take him aside and say, "Give it up." For those who doubt the hurricane was predictable, several examples of dissenting voices are provided at the end of the book. These mavericks were shouted down, excluded from lunchroom chatter, threatened, fired, and ridiculed at the turn of the millennium, but mainstream opinion has since veered sharply in their direction. We could have included many more dissenters, but then we would have had to change the subtitle.

Amazingly, most of our rogues are still at it. Although just as chameleons change color to survive, many have morphed into ambassadors of caution to better suit the country's mood, chastising others while conveniently ignoring their own cheerleading or lobbying past. And while we must all share some responsibility for the insanity of the late '90s, let's remember that the prosecutors at Nuremberg didn't go after the average guy swept up in a mania. They went after the kingpins. And since we evidently no longer have a federal system of justice based on equality, all we can do is try to shame the kingpins in lowbrow literature. Sad, isn't it?

Before we get started, in the unlikely event that you are still indoctrinated in the "averaging down your costs and avoiding panic selling" mantra that those bozos on TV or the White House lawn keep repeating endlessly, tunelessly, day after day, hour after hour, let's get a little historical perspective on our bubble. Notice the graph. It's the Dow Jones from 1929 until today. First of all, it is not really a bubble. Bubbles are round and soft. They float. And they don't have bottoms. Cliffs have bottoms. Cliffs have bottoms that are hard, flat, and cold, and they're a long way down.

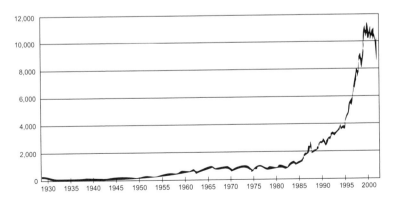

Sort of like looking at Earth from space, isn't it?

❧

A word on our ways. The job titles we list are taken from the time of the quotation. Many of these people have since moved to other companies, resigned, or disappeared. The quotations we highlight are randomly sourced, meaning that our source might not be their press debut. Many of these quotations were repeated hundreds of times across the country, adding to the buy-and-hold chorus. We also include quotations from different media outlets. The sources for these are listed in the back. The graphs are linear, based on closing prices, and with a few exceptions start from the day of the quotation and go until September 2002. They have been adjusted to reflect splits. And while some of this story line may have changed since we wrote it, this book should still give you a pretty good sense of the plot. We expect that there will be more arrests, more investigations, more bankruptcies, more settlements, more jobs lost, and more stupid statements. Of course that last one, reader, will be for you to judge.

And now, without further ado, here they are: your 1990s Stock Mania All-Stars!

ALAN GREENSPAN
Chairman, Federal Reserve Board/Knight

CP Photo Archive: Andre Forget

The stock market, as best as I can judge, is high. It's not that there is a bubble in there.

—*Federal Reserve meeting, May 1996*

AFTERMATH: Former Fed governor and now Bush adviser Lawrence Lindsey pushes Greenspan to act. In late 1996 Greenspan finally admits, "I recognize there is a stock bubble problem at this point." They don't call him a genius for nothing.

BUBBLE CLUES: From 1972 the Dow took fifteen years to double, from 1,000 to 2,000. From 1994, it doubled from 4,000 to 8,000 in three and a half years. More clues? Our building janitor watching CNBC in the broom closet and his Labrador retriever's account at Charles Schwab. Still, Greenspan uses none of the Fed's bubble-bursting tools for years. "Irrational exuberance" speech aside, he argues that economic gains reflect Internet-related innovation and productivity. In other words, he and his briefcase Toto are swept up in the mania.

BULL! For his incredible ability to spot a bubble much later than everyone else and his courage to do nothing about it, Greenspan is knighted by the Queen of England in 2002. In all likelihood she felt a kinship with a man who, for years, sat on a throne and did nothing except make the occasional speech. Although, when you think about it, she had fewer people bowing down to her.

⇒≡ **BOTTOM LINE** ≡⇐
Greenspan, as best we can judge, is high.

BILL CLINTON
President

CP Photo Archive: Ryan Remiorz

His devotion to new technologies has been so significant, I've been thinking of taking Alan.com public; then, we can pay the debt off even before 2015.

—Alan Greenspan renomination ceremony, Oval Office, January 4, 2000

AFTERMATH: Laughter erupts in the Rose Garden. The joke could probably still get a laugh today for different reasons, since the idea of dot coms as a quick way to make money has become a standard punch line.

BULL! The concept that Alan Greenspan is the only reason anyone has food and shelter is echoed by Senator John McCain in late 1999: "If Mr. Greenspan should happen to die, God forbid, I would do like we did in the movie *Weekend at Bernie's*, I would prop him up and put a pair of dark glasses on him and keep him as long as we could." As pathetic as that makes our economic miracle sound, it certainly is a hip reference for an old man.

BONUS QUOTE: In 2001, Larry King weighs in on Greenspan's indispensability: "Hopefully he doesn't nick himself shaving tomorrow." It's the Queen's dubbing sword he needs to worry about.

⇥ **BOTTOM LINE** ⇤

Okay, guys, we've propped him up for a couple of years now. Starting to stink. What next?

AL GORE
Vice President

CP Photo Archive: Ann Heisenfelt

AFTERMATH:

CP Photo Archive: Victoria Arocho

I have seen the New Economy; and I am here to tell you that it works.

—Challenge, *July 17, 1998*

MARY MEEKER

Queen of the Internet/Managing Director, Morgan Stanley Dean Witter

Grow, grow, grow, spend, spend, spend, expand, grow, spend more, grow more, and then suddenly reap the financial benefits.

—*Report on Amazon, 1998*

AFTERMATH: Trees don't grow to the sky, but that doesn't stop Meeker from fertilizing them. In May, 2001 *Fortune* demotes the Queen of the Internet to the Cover Girl of Bubblemania, reporting that Meeker still refuses to downgrade her stocks. At least she's consistent.

THE RESULT: Meeker and Morgan Stanley are named in a lawsuit brought by shareholders who, according to Bloomberg News, claim that she "offered biased research and slanted investment advice about eBay and Seattle-based Amazon as a way to secure lucrative banking business." Or, as *Fortune* puts it, "She may be the greatest dealmaker around. The problem is, she's supposed to be an analyst." Unlike Henry Blodget, Meeker decides not to settle out of court.

VERDICT: Not guilty

BULL! Meeker complains: "I'm tired of the witch-hunt, punching-bag stuff. The other side of the story never seems to get told." We're confused. Is that the part where you rate Yahoo! a buy as it falls from $100 to $9 or the part where you tell the government that you're "unavailable" when they invite you to testify?

It ain't easy being Queen.

KENNETH LAY
Chairman, Enron

I've learned that a lot of things that initially looked to me to be unreachable, undoable, or maybe even unwise, turned out to be brilliant.

—as quoted by E. A. Tilney, Enron Senior Vice President, House Subcommittee on Oversight and Investigations, May 20, 1998

AFTERMATH: Sometimes they just turn out to be unwise.

BULL! After the infamous limited partnerships and accounting methods are examined in public, Enron goes into PR mode. Over at Andersen, Nancy Temple edits out the infamous "misleading" that jurors later say convinced them of Andersen's guilt. Lay announces third-quarter results but doesn't bother to mention that the over half-billion-dollar "one-time" loss derives from what the SEC describes as "a series of complex hedging transactions" involving the CFO, Andrew Fastow. Lay does, however, mention that shareholder equity will be lowered by $1.2 billion due to an accounting error. Translation: Enron put $1.2 billion in the wrong column and Andersen looked the other way. In the next week, Lay tries to calm employees and analysts, despite rumors that the SEC is investigating Fastow. He says Fastow is doing "an outstanding job." According to the *Washington Post*, one concerned employee says, "I'd like to know if you're on crack." The next day Lay announces that Fastow is taking "a leave of absence." In December, Enron files for Chapter 11 protection.

⇒ **BOTTOM LINE** ⇐
Other times they turn out to be illegal.

LOU DOBBS

Host, CNN, Lou Dobbs Moneyline

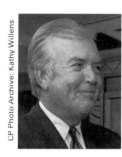

CP Photo Archive: Kathy Willens

Let me make it very clear. I'm a bull, I'm a bull, on the market, on the economy—and let me repeat, I am a bull!

—Moneyline,
August 2, 2001

AFTERMATH: In less than a year, the Dow and the NASDAQ each lose about a third of their value. Let me repeat, a third of their value!

STRATEGY: Continue to champion the robust economic recovery until the recovery is clearly as phony as his ginger hair color.

BULL! On July 31, 2002, Dobbs makes an on-air apology for embracing the Commerce Department's rosy economic projections: "The market can humble the most cautious forecaster." This raises the question Which part of "I'm a bull, on the market, on the economy—and let me repeat, I am a bull!" denotes caution?

BONUS QUOTE: Dobbs 1997: "I have a great deal of respect for Bernie Ebbers because he's tripled the market cap of WorldCom since the beginning of the year."

LOU DOBBS

Host, *CNN*, Lou Dobbs Moneyline

CP Photo Archive: Denis Doyle

We've got a cultural problem here. It extends from Wall Street, where too many people were taking shortcuts and committing outright fraud. It's occurring in corporate America, again, outright fraud and criminal behavior.

— *CNN*, Connie Chung Tonight, *July 9, 2002*

AFTERMATH: Critic Diane Holloway reviews the show: "A program on corporate scandals was especially good, with Lou Dobbs contributing cogent analysis," and the country wonders whether it's being gaslit.

BULL! Maybe Holloway isn't familiar with 1999 Dobbs: "At the same time all of this explosion in online trading is going on—and truly a revolution is under way—the chairman of the SEC, Arthur Levitt, is admonishing everyone to be very careful in their trading. He is calling for constraint; he is calling for review, talking about day traders. One could almost imagine this anarchist in the world financial system." And this one: "SEC Chairman Arthur Levitt said he is concerned that analysts are talking up stocks to hold on to the lucrative business from the companies they follow. Levitt said a study showed that only 1 percent of analysts' recommendations are to sell, while 68 percent are to buy. So far they appear to have been right." So far doesn't look as good as it once did. The new Dobbs? "It's a cultural issue that has got to be rectified now. The president can't do it by himself, nor can Congress, but they certainly can set a tone in leadership." Notably, he does not call them Anarchists.

⇒ **BOTTOM LINE** ⇐

Sweet Lou. Bends with the wind.
Offers opinions instead of analysis.

JAMES CRAMER

Host, *CNBC*, Kudlow and Cramer/*Author*, You Got Screwed

TheStreet.com

Don't confuse valuation, fan-o-mine, with my ownership. Our techs are all overvalued, but that's not a factor right now.

—Yahoo! Chat, February 10, 2000

AFTERMATH: Cramer discovers valuations on July 24, 2002: "I think that we are entering an era of sharply lower valuations and one handy-dandy series of metrics for all stocks, notably price-to-earnings ratios and dividends." Timely advice—just two years into the market crash.

MORE GENIUS-O-HIS: Asked in February 2000 for five stocks to hold for the next five years, Cramer serves up this dog's breakfast: "Yahoo!, AOL, SUNW, NOK, CSCO." Halfway through the five-year term, those who "invested" $1,000 in these stocks are left with $130. That figure is slightly overstated thanks to rounding. Even then, that $130 is largely eaten up by commissions.

BULL! To Cramer's credit, in 2000 he backs his enthusiasm for the Internet by forgoing his hefty salary at TheStreet.com for stock options. Shares in the company quickly melt down from $20 to low single digits, rendering the options worthless and Cramer's columns voluntary.

Written for free, Cramer's insights finally reach proper valuation.

JAMES CRAMER

Host, CNBC, Kudlow and Cramer/*Author,* You Got Screwed

Sun Microsystems

SUNW probably has the best near-term outlook of any company I know.

—Yahoo! Chat, September 7, 2000

AFTERMATH: SUNW (Sun Microsystems) shares go from $60 to $30 within four months, to $10 within a year, and below $3 within two years. In fairness, that may have been the best near-term outlook of any company he knew.

STRATEGY TO COMBAT DOWNTURN: After it dives to $40 in November 2000, Cramer insists: "I like SUNW!" It quickly plunges again, but after a tiny bounce above $30 he declares: "The worst is indeed over . . . you must be invested." You must be kidding.

FUTURE PLANS: By August 2001, a seemingly reborn Cramer is denouncing the tech sector and its promoters: "For too long we have allowed tech bulls to come on television or in print and talk unimpeded about how all is well. Now I am gunning for them." Isn't that like Bill Clinton gunning for adulterers?

BONUS QUOTE: "Global Crossing is a good stock." —August 24, 2000

⇒ **BOTTOM LINE** ⇒
James and the Giant Reach.

STEPHAN PATERNOT

Founder, theglobe.com

theglobe.com

Got the girl, got the money, now I'm ready to live a disgusting, frivolous life.

—*CNN*, Movers with Jan Hopkins, *July 24, 1998*

AFTERMATH: The IPO for theglobe.com, touted as "the hottest initial public stock sale offering in U.S. history," gets merchant bankers' attention, setting off a new wave of Internet offerings. Paternot describes the day as "the most euphoric moment of our lives, where our stock shot up from $9 a share up to $97." The stock loses 50 percent in the next week.

AWARD SPEECH: "You should always keep going. You should never give up, because you never know how far you can go in life."—New York Young Entrepreneur of the Year Award

BULL! Paternot and his partner Todd Krizelman are feted at parties and profiled in fawning media interviews. All this for a site that allows web users to set up their own web pages— free. On August 8, 2001, theglobe.com declares bankruptcy.

BONUS FACT: In 2002, *Fortune* reports that Paternot produced and starred in a film about an artist who paints donuts.

Paints donuts and sells investors the holes.

SCOTT SULLIVAN
CFO, WorldCom

CP Photo Archive: Kathy Willens

There is nothing dull about a story that has a solid financial picture and strategic performance.

—CFO: The Magazine for Senior Financial Executives, *September 1998*

AFTERMATH: In a later *Business Week* article, Sullivan sounds less confident: "These are challenging times and we do not take them lightly. But there are no triggers out there that would call for the repayment of debt." Four months later Sullivan is fired and WorldCom is bankrupt.

BULL! Here's how the *Business Week* article ends: "'WorldCom is still the fastest-growing telecom mega-cap company,' says Blake Bath, a telecom analyst at Lehman Brothers. 'While it's hardly in the clear, WorldCom is no Global Crossing.'" Have they stopped teaching skepticism in journalism school?

BULL! 1998 CFO Excellence Award.

TRUE STRATEGIC PERFORMANCE: David Myers, former WorldCom controller, in Federal District Court, Manhattan, decides that it is in his interests to cooperate with the authorities: "I was instructed on a quarterly basis by senior management to ensure that entries were made to falsify WorldCom's reported actual costs and, therefore, to increase WorldCom's reported earnings." Sullivan's trial is set for September 2003.

⇥ **BOTTOM LINE** ⇤
Nothing dull about that story.

GARY WINNICK
Founder and Chairman, Global Crossing

Associated Press: Dennis Cook

We're not going to be the Flying Wallendas in the business. We have a big responsibility to our share-holder base and to our employees. And, uh, we're never going to violate that.

—*As reported by PBS, 1999*

AFTERMATH: Global Crossing makes every high-flying list of the bubble, adding Andersen and Salomon Smith Barney for fuel. Jack Grubman cheerleads. Debts grow to $12 billion, and CEOs enter and exit while the market shrinks. Global shares move from their $61 high to zero.

STRATEGY TO COMBAT DOWNTURN: Lay off thousands, seek Chapter 11, refuse offer of $750 million, but, eight months later, accept offer of $250 million from same buyer. Despite problems, do not resign.

BULL! By cashing in $735 million in options and demanding perks and consulting fees while the company goes bankrupt, Winnick adds to his $4 to $6 billion fortune, making him one of the richest men in America. Meanwhile, the 886 million Global Crossing shares are near worthless. In October 2002, Winnick offers $25 million to employees who lost in their 401(k)s. "The only legacy I am going to leave this planet with is my name." No, Gary, that's gone now. And you can't buy a new one.

BONUS QUOTE: "I know I can go back to anonymity in a quick minute. It doesn't take much to fall off a rock." Or crawl back under one.

TIM TINDALL

Reporter, CNBC, Business News

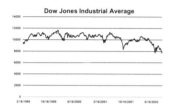

AFTERMATH: Dow credibility under stress but not because of tech stocks.

BULL! In February 2001, Tindall is included in a round of layoffs at CNBC.

The explosive growth of the tech sector is threatening to undermine the credibility of the one-hundred-year-old [Dow] index, and increasingly, more professional and individual investors are questioning its relevance.

—*CNBC*, The Fast Track: Intelligent Investing, *February 15, 1999*

Switch "CNBC" for "one-hundred-year-old index" and re-read the quotation.

RALPH ACAMPORA

Senior Technical Analyst, Prudential Securities/Author,
The Fourth Mega-Market

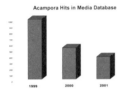

Acampora Hits in Media Database

1999   2000   2001

I'm not saying this is a straight line up. I'm not saying you can't have pauses. I'm saying any kind of decline, buy them.

—*CNN,* Moneyline *News Hour, December 23, 1999*

AFTERMATH: Acampora's prediction of a 14,000 Dow by the end of 2000 crashes and burns at a most inopportune time. He had just released a book predicting another eleven years for the bull market.

STRATEGY: The acclaimed "media hero" goes underground. A database search of "Acampora" turns up almost 1,000 entries for 1999, but just 524 for 2000 and 373 for 2001. Ron Carter of the *Columbus Dispatch* writes: "The silence is troubling."

BULL! Acampora later explains his faulty projection for 2000: "I'm a trend follower, and last year most of the indicators were going up. The techs had momentum, the Dow had momentum, and everyone was enthusiastic." Thanks, that's really helpful.

=== **BOTTOM LINE** ===

If Acampora sees his shadow when he comes out of his hole, it's another six months of bear markets.

RALPH ACAMPORA

Senior Technical Analyst, Prudential Securities/Author, The Fourth Mega-Market

Dow Jones Industrial Average

I'm so pumped. [Dow 10,000] is wonderful . . . I think that what is propelling this market are two things—one is peace and the other one is technology.

—BBC World Service, March 20, 1999

AFTERMATH: Despite the continued presence of technological advancement and peace, the Dow is back to 10,000 over two years later and is in a sharp downtrend when it hits 9,431 on September 10, 2001.

BULL! Acampora on that same day in 1999: "When you have companies like General Electric and Johnson & Johnson and Citigroup—this is blue-chip America at work. If it were very speculative stocks, I would worry. I am not worried about the quality of the leadership." A few years later, GE would be 35 percent lower, Citigroup would be under investigation for its role in the Enron and WorldCom scandals, and it would be clear that even blue chips can be bid up to maniacal levels when enough Acamporas get "pumped."

BONUS QUOTE: "The year 2000 is a presidential election year—the Dow usually has a good ending in a presidential election year." This is one step above astrology.

(Austrian accent) "We're not here to analyze. We are here to pump (clap) you up."

RALPH ACAMPORA

Senior Technical Analyst, Prudential Securities/Author, The Fourth Mega-Market

The reasons for the mega-market—peace, new technology, optimism, the aging of the baby boomers—have not changed.

—The Fourth Mega-Market, *1999*

AFTERMATH: Three years later, the baby boomers are still aging.

BULL! Ongoing peace is Acampora's number-one reason to anticipate a bull run right through to 2011. While many argue that the 9/11 attack was completely unpredictable, Osama bin Laden had already declared war on America; terrorists had already bombed the USS *Cole*, two embassies in Africa, and even the World Trade Center. These are clues a deep macro thinker who contemplates seventeen-year patterns could have latched on to. Or he could've just watched *Nightline*, which reported extensively on the prospect of a serious domestic attack.

BONUS QUOTE: "Peace is bullish." The Great Depression occurred in peacetime.

GERHARD SCHMID

CEO and Founder, MobilCom

In the traditional way of thinking, there would have been no place on the stock market for a company like ours. We're too young.

—London Financial Times, *March 27, 1999*

AFTERMATH: MobilCom, a German telecom, is the first company to go public on the Neuer Markt, a new German market closely designed after the NASDAQ. MobilCom quickly takes on huge losses and, in fall 2002, asks the German government for a bail out. Now there's a cold call you wouldn't want to make . . . Hello, Chancellor, I need $391 million.

BULL! On September 25, 2002, the Neuer Markt closes for business, down 95 percent from its peak. The remaining stocks are transferred to more traditional markets.

RICHARD GRASSO

Chairman, NYSE

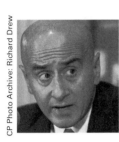

CP Photo Archive: Richard Drew

It's [Dow 10,000] really not a Wall Street event, it's a Main Street event; 200 million Americans are benefiting by what's just happened.

—*CNBC*, Dow 10,000 Special, *March 29, 1999*

AFTERMATH: The Dow retraces to 1998 levels as Main Street discovers who was really benefiting: Ken Lay, Jack Grubman, and Martha Stewart.

BULL! In the post-10,000 celebration, Grasso and Rudy Giuliani hurl hats emblazoned with "Dow 10,000" into the NYSE throng. Curiously, one year later, there are no hats dispensed when the Dow hits 10,000 on the way down.

CLOSING CREDITS: Grasso thanks the public for Dow 10,000: "I want to send thank yous to the 70 million Americans who participate directly in equities and another 130 million who participate indirectly." Now that those same Americans are stampeding out of equities, will Grasso be sending them thanks-for-nothing cards?

⊷ **BOTTOM LINE** ⊶
Every casino needs a greeter.

HARRY S. DENT

Best-selling Author, The Roaring 2000s

CP Photo Archive: Denis Doyle

AFTERMATH: When people start getting excited about Flooz, which provides an alternate (e)currency, and Pets.com, which sends cat litter through the mail, bears realize that there is a paradigm shift all right, but it's not the one Dent is talking about.

STRATEGY TO COMBAT DOWNTURN: Write another book: *The Greatest Bull Market in History, 2003–2008.*

BULL! Dent's bullish forecasts are based on the demographics of the boomers' life cycle and the Internet "paradigm shift," a.k.a. the New Economy. To his credit, Dent does foresee that, despite dot-com flops, the Internet will revolutionize many sectors, including secondhand book stores.

[Bears] have studied past performances and say the market is out of whack. They are not realizing there has been a paradigm shift.

—Baltimore Sun,
March 30, 1999

⇥ **BOTTOM LINE** ⇤
The Roaring 2000s currently selling for $0.40 online. S & H extra.

LARRY WACHTEL

Market Analyst, Prudential Securities

Nasdaq Composite

When people say the market is over-valued and there's a bubble, whatever that means, they're talking about just a hand-ful of stocks. Most of these stocks are reasonably priced. There's no reason for them to correct violently anytime in the year 2000.

—*CNN,* Moneyline, *December 23, 1999*

AFTERMATH: The NASDAQ loses 50 percent of its value in a violent correction in the year 2000. But there's no concern if you have a savvy veteran like Wachtel managing your money, because he's bound to recognize the danger early on.

MARCH 16, 2000: "I would not abandon in any way, shape, or form the technology group. It just got overextended; this is a correction. We saw the same thing in January, we saw two 10 percent pullbacks in the NASDAQ and we went on; so, that is the nature of the beast."

BULL! At the end of 2000, Wachtel predicts the NASDAQ will be at 3,000 in a year. Not even close.

NEW STRATEGY: Wachtel's stock market advice in June 2002: "Pray."

➻ **BOTTOM LINE** ➻
Now you know what a bubble means, Larry.

GEORGE GILDER

Author, Gilder Technology Report

JDS Uniphase

[JDS Uniphase is] the Intel of the Telecosm.

—Chief Executive, *May 1999*

AFTERMATH: The technology-spiritualist guru is right. Uniphase follows Intel on a sharp run then falls on knife, but the JDS knife is deadlier. It cuts all the way to $2.

BULL! Gilder's newsletter, the *Gilder Technology Report*, is a $300 a year heady mix of futurist-visionary predictions and stock picks with a great track record. But as stocks fail, Gilder leads the buy-and-hold cheer. Six months after the tech crash, TheStreet.com quotes a post from a Gilder message board: "[He's] still telling us that Global Crossing, Globalstar, WorldCom and others still boast great technology and good management." They quote another Gilderism, "If the judgment of the report is correct, your current qualms will seem insignificant." When you're trying to save your house from foreclosure, Wall Street must seem pretty far away.

CAPITULATION: Gilder tells *Wired* in July 2002: "I accepted the laurels when they were being offered. Now I really have to eat crow and not skulk off to a corner and claim 'I'm just a technologist.'"

≒ **BOTTOM LINE** ≕

Gilder is the Pet Rock of the Telecosm.

RICHARD THOMAN

CEO, Xerox

CP Photo Archive: Stephen Chernin

[Xerox] is poised on the threshold of another period of great success.

—*Shareholders annual meeting, May 20, 1999*

AFTERMATH: During Thoman's tenure Xerox drops from $70 to $25 a share. He is fired less than a year later.

PACKAGE: $800,000 in pension. A year. Every year. For the rest of his life. He was CEO for thirteen months. As shares continue to fall, Thoman develops neck problems from looking over his shoulder.

NEXT! Paul Allaire, who was CEO before Thoman, returns and allegedly bullies the KPMG partner in charge of Xerox and the balance sheet.

NEXT! Anne Mulcahy is named CEO with this stellar recommendation: "The plan called for a gradual transition of leadership with Anne becoming CEO when the board was confident of the effective execution of Xerox's turnaround. Clearly, this requirement has been met." Shares are now at $8. Clearly, in the New Economy, $25 to $8 is a turnaround.

BULL! In April 2002, Xerox agrees to pay a $10 million SEC fine for Allaire's indiscretions. Then, U.S. attorneys decide they want to take a look. Shares shimmy under $6.

━━ **BOTTOM LINE** ━━

Xerox . . . spitting out CEOs and printing its own balance sheet.

BILL GRIFFETH

Anchor, CNBC

Dow Jones Industrial Average

You know, now that the Dow has passed the 10,000 mark, what do investors do with their portfolios? The easy answer to the question is nothing.

—*CNBC*, Dow 10,000
Special, *March 29, 1999*

AFTERMATH: Dow 7,500.

BULL! Long term, it's somewhat possible that investors who just hold on to their stocks beyond 1999 will see decent rates of return. There is no question that those who recognize overvaluation, go to cash, and buy back in after the massive correction will do better whether they pick the bottom or not.

LOOK WHO'S SQUAWKING: In September 2000, *Squawk Box* host Mark Haines tells *Nightline*: "There are an awful lot of people out there who are a lot better off as a result of watching CNBC." He's probably referring to the 2001 episode where they air sportscaster Dick Enberg's views on the tech stocks: "I'm very confident that this market is about to bottom out and then move ahead."

⇥ **BOTTOM LINE** ⇤
CNBC's easy answers gradually give way to hard facts.

DAVID ELIAS

Money Manager/Author, The Dow 40,000 Portfolio

We wanted to get investor expectations down and we wanted to come up with a number that was a done deal. The real question is whether it's going to 50,000, 60,000 or 70,000.

—Buffalo News, *September 26, 1999*

AFTERMATH: After its incredible journey up, the Dow begins its incredible journey down to below 8,000. Elias's prediction of an average 9 percent gain in the market doesn't look quite as effortless as it once did.

BULL! Elias defends his picks: "I think the market is giving us an opportunity to buy some of these world class companies at significantly reduced prices." After the Internet crash in April 2000, Elias says, "There's a high probability it could go lower, but if you're a long-term investor, three or five years from now you won't even remember this." Very true. Memories of the 2000 tech crash have already been erased by memories of the 2001 and 2002 crashes.

DENNIS KOZLOWSKI

CEO, Tyco International

There are no restatements coming from Tyco, no irregularities, no investigations nor reasons for any investigations.

—Bloomberg News, *October 14, 1999*

AFTERMATH: And there's no art in my town house! Tyco drops from $43.50 to below $10.

BULL! Despite a three-year $322 million salary, three company houses worth over $30 million, an $11 million furniture budget, and a $6,000 shower curtain, Kozlowski allegedly tries to dodge New York sales tax on $15 million worth of flower paintings by shipping empty boxes to Tyco HQ in New Hampshire and forwards the art to his New York apartment.

THE TROUBLE WITH TYCO: After surviving an informal 1999 SEC inquiry into its accounting methods, Tyco is subject to another look-see after Kozlowski is indicted on the tax evasion charges. Even Tyco eventually sues Kozlowski. New York prosecutors charge him with "looting" and freeze $600 million related to the fraud charges.

BONUS FACT: When Kozlowski can't make bail, his ex-wife puts up $10 million to keep him out of Rikers, thereby raising the stock of first wives everywhere.

⊰⊱ **BOTTOM LINE** ⊰⊱
There are no shower curtains in prison.

JAMIE KIGGEN

Analyst, CS First Boston, formerly of DLJ

In our view it's crazy to get off this train heading into the holiday shopping season. Do you really want to bet against Amazon as they make a massive bet on Q4? We don't. And more evidence of Amazon's model should become apparent as year 2000 unfolds.

—TheStreet.com, October 28, 1999

AFTERMATH: Days after Kiggen defends his "top pick" rating and his $140 price target, his employer, DLJ, helps manage Amazon's $600 million bond deal. Kiggen continues to defend his $140 target by explaining that, according to his calculations, each customer will spend an average of $2,400 a year. If that weren't enough to convince skeptical investors, in December 2000 Kiggen goes undercover at the Amazon warehouse for two days to prove that the company will make its fourth-quarter sales.

BULL! The *American Prospect* reports that even if Kiggen's figures weren't "ludicrously high . . . it would have meant no profit for the company until the year 2030." Kiggen survives a complaint lodged against him at the National Association of Securities Dealers, which takes no action. Later, the Massachusetts Secretary of the Commonwealth names Kiggen in a securities-fraud-analyst-tainting case against CSFB when they discover e-mails that allegedly discuss keeping Kiggen's Yahoo! rating at hold although it "should probably be at a sell."

⊷≡ BOTTOM LINE ≡⊶

Next stop? Six months down the line . . . Amazon 31 percent lower.

26

JAMIE KIGGEN

Analyst, CS First Boston, formerly of DLJ

DLJ's Jamie Kiggen reits *buy* [GoTo.com] and raises price target from $100 to $160 after strong Q4 earnings report.

—Briefing.com, February 15, 2000

AFTERMATH: Even with the announcement of Kiggen's price target, GoTo.com closes $9 lower, at $83. It is getting late in the Internet game, and the media and investors are weary. By July 2001, the stock hits a new low of $10, but Kiggen maintains his rating. By now, we assume you've already guessed that DLJ underwrote the GoTo.com IPO.

BULL! In late December 2001, long after the bubble deflates, Kiggen chides investors in the *New York Times*: "Using the fact of a price target as a substitute for analysis if you're an investor is dangerous." Apparently that advice applies to analysts, too. Kiggen leaves CSFB in 2002 but a lawsuit keeps his name in the business section.

BONUS FACT: CFSB pays $100 million fine to the NASD and SEC to settle what the NASD release calls their "IPO profit-sharing practice."

CHARLES KADLEC

Investment Strategist, Seligman/Author, Dow 100,000: Fact or Fiction

Projected U.S. Web Users 1994-2002

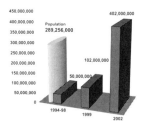

Within four years, 50 million people in the United States had "been on the Web." During 1999, the number of people using the Internet doubled to 102 million. That number is expected to double and then double again by 2002.

—Weekend Australian,
November 20, 1999

AFTERMATH: Kadlec's prediction that 408 million Americans would take to the Internet in 2002 proves wrong, as the total American population is under 300 million.

INTERNET MADNESS: During the same rant about the Internet revolution, Kadlec chirps: "Schwab, one of the leaders in providing online brokerage services, now has a higher market value than Merrill Lynch." By 2002, Schwab's market value slumps to a third of Merrill Lynch's.

BULL! Kadlec's "Dow 100,000" prediction is based heavily on the idea that people on the Internet are infinitely more productive. Yes, there's really nothing more productive than a nation of people instant-messaging their friends and downloading porn all day.

⇾ **BOTTOM LINE** ⇽

Sorry, no bottom line for this one. Playing computer *Jeopardy!* against a guy in the Netherlands.

CHARLES KADLEC

Investment Strategist, Seligman/Author, Dow 100,000: Fact or Fiction

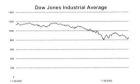

I expect it [Dow 100,000] around 2020. But it's really a metaphor for the great prosperity ahead. The big risk is being mesmerized by the short term and not seeing this long term opportunity.

—Business Week,
December 27, 1999

AFTERMATH: The Dow does a sideways act for most of the next two years, beginning a serious correction in 2001.

STRATEGY TO COMBAT DOWNTURN: In late 2001 Kadlec moves the Dow 100,000 target date back to 2023 with this hedge: "From where we stand today it's a very reasonable expectation but far from guaranteed."

BULL! Kadlec's original proposition would mean a tenfold Dow increase in twenty-one years. Problem is, the 10,000 level in 1999 was basically a market top. After the 1929 market top, it took sixty-two years to grow by ten times. After the much less lofty 1966 peak, it still took thirty-three years.

BOTTOM LINE

Charles Kadlec is one of the most underappreciated fiction writers of his time.

BARBRA STREISAND
Superstar

CP Photo Archive: Trudeau

I'm up 89 percent today on my account since August 31!

—Fortune, *June 21, 1999*

AFTERMATH: As the year wears on, Streisand and the press clash over whether her investments in high-profile stocks like AOL and eBay have led to subsequent losses. Streisand insists that her returns are positive but is no longer specific with her percentages.

BULL! According to the *Fortune* article, Streisand had a "real time stock quote service" installed in her home, she "watches CNBC, religiously," and "she wakes up at 6:30 every morning to catch the opening of the East Coast stock markets." This behavior began in 1998, and there's no record of it in the media after 2000. Stock mania, textbook case. It keeps her from making any movies in the late '90s, though, so nobody's complaining.

MARKET CALL: During the craze, Streisand allegedly makes personal phone calls to the Internet analyst Mary Meeker, CNBC's Joe Kernen, and TheStreet.com's CEO, Kevin English. They may even have knocked the Democratic National Committee off her speed dial for a few months.

⇌ **BOTTOM LINE** ⇌

Everyone was up 89 percent in the middle of 1999. And this proves it.

KEN KURSON

Writer/Founder, Green

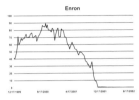
Enron

AFTERMATH: Did you hear that? It's the sound of pixie dust settling.

BULL! In a profile, Kurson, who has written for *Worth*, *Green*, and *Esquire* and who now writes for *Money*, told the *New York Times*, "I definitely love money, but I'm more intellectually fascinated by how it works than I am interested in walking through piles of it barefoot." He also tells the *Times* that "I don't appreciate irony." That's too bad, because you'd think a guy who is "intellectually fascinated" by how money works might see that there is a problem with taking advice from investment banks and their coworkers. In 2002, Kurson backtracks slightly in *Money*, "The key is to focus on the raw information, not the earnings estimate or the buy, sell or hold advice."

Everyone listens to Abby Joseph Cohen. Goldman Sachs makes a large percentage of its money from its actual investing. So if that institution owns some of the stock you like, that's a good endorsement.

—CNNfn, December 15, 1999

BONUS FACT: AJC, to whom "everyone listens," lists Enron as one of her 2001 stock picks in *Money*.

Not ironic. Just hilarious.

FORTUNE

Consumer magazine

CP Photo Archive: Denis Doyle

As the Internet broadens from the realm of geeks to encompass much of business, how do you track its performance? Here's our proposal: an index of e-stocks with the potential to upstage the Dow.

—December 6, 1999

AFTERMATH: Needless to say, most of the e-50 stocks lose well over half their value in the ensuing three years. Moreover, by early 2002 only twenty-two of the companies are profitable, and only four pay a dividend over 1 percent.

BULL! In that 1999 introduction to the e-50, *Fortune* says, "For all the upheaval the Internet has caused . . . it's nothing compared with what's to come." Have to give them that one.

INTERESTING FOOTNOTE: To help give the list some weight, they include some "old economy" type companies that are shifting into Internet areas. One is WorldCom, another the now hobbling AT&T. The other telecom singled out in the introduction: Global Crossing. Did *e* stand for extinct?

✢⇒ **BOTTOM LINE** ⇒✢
The Dow won't be upstaged by the e-50. There's still something compelling about food, shelter, and transportation.

DAVID RYNECKI

Staff Writer, Fortune

CP Photo Archive: Denis Doyle

Though it's unfair to pin all the blame for crashing stock prices on research analysts, there's no question that a large number of investors feel burned by the very people they were counting on for information. And in truth, they were burned—by shoddy research.

—Fortune, *June 11, 2001*

AFTERMATH: Rynecki then introduces *Fortune*'s List of All-Star Analysts without questioning whether investors feel burned by *Fortune*, *Forbes*, and *Fast Company* among others, who offered sexy profiles of Wall Street's Top Everyone with a Desk, Dick, or Calculator.

BULL! "The final years of the late bull market, we now know, were less about spreading new-economy virtues than about old-fashioned boosterism." That's quite an accusation from a guy who opened his July 2000 profile of Jack Grubman with "Call him the Insider." Even when Rynecki questions Grubman's conflicts, he sounds more like Terry Bradshaw: "But can Grubman cultivate that inside game and retain his credibility among investors?" When Grubman touts WorldCom as "dirt cheap," Rynecki doesn't mention WorldCom's relationship with Salomon Smith Barney. Shoddy research, boosterism, or both? As for the vaunted *Fortune* lists, they proliferated with WorldCom, Lay, Skilling et al. and resulted in more press releases, interviews, and coronations, all adding to the rah-rah atmosphere.

⊰ **BOTTOM LINE** ⊱

Top American Cheerleaders.

RICH KARLGAARD

Publisher, Forbes ASAP

Associated Press: Ho

How do you play Gilder for stocks? . . . Easy answer! Cobble together your own portfolio consisting of Gilder Telecosm stocks, hedged by instruments of your own liking.

—Forbes, *April 3, 2000*

AFTERMATH: Two weeks later the tech market collapses.

BULL! Karlgaard ends his column with a plug worthy of QVC: "And, oh yes—George Gilder. You can order his superb monthly newsletter for $295 by calling . . . or by going . . . on the Web." He continues to plug Gilder through 2001. According to *Wired,* Karlgaard does not disclose that while Gilder writes the report, *Forbes* is in charge of "the publishing, marketing, distribution and the two companies . . . split the proceeds." In 2002, Gilder admits to *Wired* that he was terrified to yell sell because 50 percent of his subscribers signed up at the peak, which coincidentally would be around the time Karlgaard was promoting Gilder in *Forbes.*

BONUS FACT: *Forbes ASAP* is shut down in October 2002. According to *Forbes:* "There is no market for a dedicated New Economy publication."

BONUS QUESTION: What are the odds of a guy named Rich being the publisher of *Forbes?*

≁ **BOTTOM LINE** ≁
Caveat lector.

ANTHONY NOTO

Analyst, Goldman Sachs

CP Photo Archive: Denis Doyle

[eToys] presents an attractive investment opportunity at current levels, and the decline in its stock is unwarranted as it will likely beat our quarter revenue estimate.

—*December 6, 1999, as reported by TheStreet.com, December 17, 1999*

AFTERMATH: By June 2000 the stock is down to $6 from $57, but that doesn't stop Noto from including it on his list of e-retailers that will survive. (Seven of the eight top stocks, including eToys, were Goldman clients.) Six months later, eToys falls 73 percent in one day, from $0.75 to $0.28, when it announces that it only has enough cash for four months. Noto downgrades it from market outperform to outperform, whatever that means.

BULL! According to the *New York Times*, when Noto finally does downgrade the stocks he covers, most of which are included on his "survival" list, they've lost an average of 98.2 percent. Noto defends his position on CNN: "The market sentiment unfortunately ran away from these stocks, and caused the stocks to come down significantly. We at that time didn't change our ratings because when the stocks were down 50 to 60 percent, it didn't seem appropriate." In other words, he maintained a buy because he didn't want to be rude. That's probably a more honest assessment than he cares to admit. eToys ends 2001 by filing for Chapter 11.

⇌ **BOTTOM LINE** ⇌
www.sec.gov/complaint.shtml?

ROBERT REITZES
Portfolio Manager, Bear Stearns

Cisco

And B-to-B, I love B-to-B. I never even heard of B-to-B three weeks ago.

—CNN, Moneyweek, December 18, 1999

AFTERMATH: The term *B-to-B* fades from the daily lexicon as quickly as Reitzes fell in love with it. *BtoB* magazine's top-rated 2002 web site, 3Com, is a money loser with a stock down 96 percent. Even the successful ones, such as Perot Systems, fall 75 percent or more.

BULL! Among Reitzes's greatest hits: "The web is going to grow . . . you have to be there," "I think Cisco is like the mother ship . . . it's hard not to have this in your portfolio," and before a big drop-off in stocks in February 2001, "We've gone from a position of about 60 percent net long to about 85, 90. So that I think speaks reams."

CAPITULATION: In March 2001: "I've capitulated in the sense of admitting I have no idea what's going to go . . . everybody's just frustrated and everybody's just waiting like, what's going on." God recognizes this cry for help, so Fannie Mae—Reitzes's top stock pick that day—quickly shoots up about 60 percent.

⇒⊱ **BOTTOM LINE** ⇒⊱

Love means never having to say "I sold you."

FRED BARBASH

Investment Columnist and Business Editor, Washington Post

Cisco

I've surveyed the surveys of "best stocks" for 2000. . . . I doubt there would be much dissent about the quality of these companies as investments. The top picks are CSCO; AOL; . . . QCOM; WCOM; LU; and TXN. I suspect that if you bought a little of each now, in ten years you'd be a satisfied investor.

—Washington Post,
December 26, 1999

AFTERMATH: The big winner in the group is TXN, which still has 40 percent of its value. The other five have retained an average of 10 percent. In fairness, if they increase 1,200 percent over the next seven years, Barbash will be vindicated.

BULL! Barbash makes these casual remarks in an article about how these "best" stocks are the "safe" choices, but he says that investors should also roll the dice on riskier ones to cash in on the Internet revolution. Only two of the "safe" companies have a PE ratio under 57 in a hot economy, and only one pays the slightest dividend.

WHY MENTION BARBASH? Because seemingly nice enough guys like him, who weren't directly part of the stock-selling industry but who passed along the same mantras, kept the mania going. Thousands of Barbashes around the country could have asked skeptical questions but instead chose to become surrogate PR reps for the large-cap techs.

STRATEGY TO COMBAT DOWNTURN: Barbash retires from his column in 2001 to become a stay-at-home dad.

⇥ **BOTTOM LINE** ⇤

Still, a marked improvement over his *Post* predecessor, James Glassman.

JAMES GLASSMAN
Syndicated Columnist/Coauthor, Dow 36,000

Dow Jones Industrial Average

What is dangerous is for Americans *not* to be in the stock market. We're going to reach the point where stocks are correctly priced, and we think that's 36,000. . . . It's not just a bubble. Far from it. The stock market is undervalued.

—*CNN, Crossfire,*
December 21, 1999

AFTERMATH: Dow 7,300.

CAVEAT: Glassman's 1999 prediction that the Dow would go to 36,000 has a five-year horizon. It's therefore necessary to reserve judgment until . . . who are we kidding, is this guy a schmuck or what?

STRATEGY: Glassman continues to stand by his prediction and his book. Booksellers are also continuing to support the book, although they've moved it from the business section to humor.

BULL! Glassman continues to champion stocks as "the most reliable route to accumulating wealth." He blames the current situation not on an overexcited market but on gloom-'n'-doom naysayers. He neglects to mention that most naysayers were fired or kept off the airwaves until the Dow fell 20 percent. Talk about the power of positive thinking.

✢ **BOTTOM LINE** ✢
It's not just a bubble. It's a bubblehead.

ASH RAJAN

Senior VP of Equity Focus Group, Prudential Securities

This [Dow 10,000] tells people they can't sit back and find excuses not to be in the market. If they do, it will pass them by.

—Dallas Morning News,
March 30, 1999

AFTERMATH: Those who get passed by Dow 10,000 get six more chances to get on board over the next three years. The Dow 8,000 bus is just around the bend too.

BULL! On April 24, 2000, after the NASDAQ has begun to correct, a bewildered Rajan says, "I'm stunned at this market quite frankly." He nevertheless goes on to recommend Oracle, Qualcomm, Nokia, and the semiconductor sector. All are on the cusp of calamitous declines.

CAPITULATION: In 2001 he speaks of diversifying into defensive stocks, fixed income, and even cash. A year after that, he dismisses a developing Dow rally: "I'm not sure it'll prove sustainable."

＋≈ **BOTTOM LINE** ≈＋

Prudential has given us Acampora, Wachtel, and Rajan. In a big landslide, maybe the last thing anyone needs is a Piece of the Rock.

WALTER P. PIECYK, JR.

Analyst, Paine Webber

Qualcomm

Make the investment [Qualcomm] today and hold onto it over a period of time. We think that it will generate significantly higher returns than the market offers.

—Bloomberg News, *December 30, 1999*

AFTERMATH: On the day of Piecyk's famous call that Qualcomm would hit $1,000, the stock spikes $156, reaching a high of $717.24. It then does a 4-to-1 split and falls to the $20 range. For investors who did "make the investment today," their $10,000 would now be worth $1,500.

BULL! Two years later, TheStreet.com jokes about Piecyk: "Piecyk left Wall Street and hasn't been heard from since." No such luck. Piecyk later turns up at Fulcrum Global Partners LLC, giving a bullish forecast on Nokia in February 2002: "Nokia already has strong market share and margins in its infrastructure and handset business." Over the next six months, Nokia stock is slashed in half.

✢⟩ **BOTTOM LINE** ⟨✢

Fool me once, shame on you. Fool me twice . . .

40

JOSEPH BATTIPAGLIA

Chief Investment Strategist, Ryan Beck & Co.

Nasdaq Composite

Some fear a burst Internet bubble, but our analysis shows that Internet companies account for only 7 percent of the overall NSDQ market cap but carry expected long-term growth rates twice those of other rapidly growing segments within tech.

—Business Times,
December 31, 1999

AFTERMATH: As it sinks in that "expected" growth rates have no connection to reality, the Philadelphia Internet Index goes from its March 2000 high of 1,350 to 472 in six months.

STRATEGY: Perhaps buoyed by the index's sudden 28 percent bounce to 605, Battipaglia uncorks this winner: "I think technology is going to perform very well in the economy coming and the economy next year. The problem here, though, is there's a change of leadership. It's away from the PCcentric companies into the Internet and networking companies." The Internet index finishes the year at 300 and the following year at 192.

BULL! The forecast on September 4, 2002: "I think we've seen the lows and we're steadily going to build momentum for a stronger market." Does that inspire confidence?

ANTHONY MULLER

CFO, JDS Uniphase

JDS Uniphase

A business that has certainly stood the test of time was Levi Strauss. The guy who made the pants for the miners. . . . Advance forward 150 years to the Internet gold rush, somebody has to make the pants for the Internet. And that's our job.

—The Motley Fool, *January 24, 2000*

AFTERMATH: The JDS strategy of growing by acquisition leads to the largest write-down of all time. (Sadly, that record quickly falls, but finishing second in a write-down contest with AOL is no shame.) In a modest move, the historic loss isn't mentioned in JDS's July 2001 earnings release until paragraph 10.

STRATEGY TO COMBAT DOWNTURN: Muller defends the acquisitions as mostly noncash deals that leave JDS well positioned for the future. It's a future Muller wants no part of, since he's retiring from the company in March 2003.

BULL! When Muller thanks *Motley Fool* writer Bill Mann for that publication's long-time support, Mann says: "Well, we do like companies that we consider to be excellent for investors . . . but you all deserve credit for looking after the individual investor." Those individual investors have since launched a class action suit against JDS executives including Muller.

BONUS FACT: Levi Strauss & Co. had a patent that protected it from competition for thirty years. Otherwise, very similar.

⇜ **BOTTOM LINE** ⇝
The Internet is caught with its pants down.

BRIAN FINNERTY
Head of NASDAQ Trading, C. E. Unterberg, Towbin

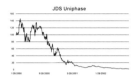

Uniphase gave us a great number yesterday. . . . JDS Uniphase is trading at two hundred times earnings. But is that overvalued? I don't know.

—CNNfn, January 27, 2000

AFTERMATH: JDS Uniphase stock goes from $200 a share to over $400, where it remains today. Just kidding; at last check it's $1.83.

TRUE VALUE: The "great number" can't be that great, because JDS has never made a yearly profit. The market considers this fact in January 2000 and assigns the company a worth of $68 billion. Overvalued? Finn's not sure.

BULL! In a vintage mania moment, when Finnerty praises JDS's acquisitions (which later result in the largest write-down of its time) and says the projected 50 percent earnings growth rate could get even bigger, the supposedly objective CNNfn anchor Lauren Thierry says, "You got that right." Somebody's got a future hosting infomercials.

➤ **BOTTOM LINE** ➤
Two things you can't put a value on—your health and optical networking equipment companies.

SAMUEL WAKSAL
CEO, ImClone

CP Photo Archive: David Karp

We believe this process will culminate with a successful approval by the FDA and that this drug will be on the market sometime next year.

—*CNN*, Lou Dobbs Moneyline, *May 14, 2001*

AFTERMATH: Close, as they say, only counts in horseshoes. On December 4, 2001, the FDA meets with ImClone, hinting that it will not approve their cancer drug Erbitux.

ALLEGED STRATEGY TO COMBAT DOWNTURN: Try to sell stock. When Merrill Lynch and Bank of America refuse to sell (Hallelujah! Someone did something according to the law), have your daughter, brother, father, and friends sell their stock. Drive stock price down 30 percent by the time the FDA announces rejection to Joe Blow investors. Get yourself arrested on June 12. When asked if you put personal profit before cancer patients, plead the Fifth Amendment. Get down on your knees and thank God for the Constitution. On October 16, 2002, plead guilty to six out of thirteen charges. "I have made terrible mistakes. . . . I was wrong."

BULL! How many millions do these people need? Surely ImClone's stock wouldn't have been, in Congressman Billy Tauzin's words, such "a train wreck" if they'd just sold their holdings along with everyone else. Certainly nobody would be doing the perp walk on the cover of every paper in the country.

⇥ **BOTTOM LINE** ⇤
Ph.D. in immunology can't protect you from your own virus.

MARTHA STEWART

CEO, Martha Stewart Living Omnimedia/Broker

MSO

Well, I don't know if I like all the mergers, but I do like all the action. I really like what's happening, the thoughtful-ness and the unthoughtfulness —it's exciting.

—*CNN*, Larry King Live, *February 2, 2000*

AFTERMATH: In 2002, Stewart tires of the action: "I just want to focus on my salad."

STRATEGY TO COMBAT DOWNTURN: Decline invitation to Washington. Curtail public appearances to spend more time with lawyer.

BULL! Stewart sells shares of her friend Sam Waksal's company ImClone on December 27, 2001, the day before the FDA announcement, net-ting $227,000. If that weren't bad enough, she and other board members are slapped with a lawsuit that alleges "Stewart and other company insiders dumped 5.3 million Omnimedia shares worth $79 million based on private information about the scandal brewing over Stewart's sales of ImClone Systems shares." Shares of Martha Stewart Omnimedia drop faster than a spoiled soufflé— down over 50 percent. Martha resigns her position on the NYSE, which was announced in March. It is worth asking whether she accepted the nomina-tion while aware of the investigation.

IS IT A GOOD THING? Critics have long complained about the risks of investing in a living brand. "If she got hit by a car, it's all over." Share-holders are considering their options.

⇥ **BOTTOM LINE** ⇤
Tasteless.

LARRY KUDLOW

Host, CNBC/Economist/Republican Adviser

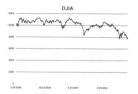

This correction will run its course until the middle of the year. Then things will turn up again, because not even Greenspan can stop the Internet economy."

—The New York Post,
February 25, 2000.

AFTERMATH: Kudlow writes of "a sizable stock-market bounce yet to come" on March 6, 2002, right before the Dow plunges another 20 percent.

STRATEGY TO COMBAT DOWNTURN: Blame Greenspan for stopping the Internet economy: "If you really want to know the biggest reason for the stock-market-led business recession that came to an end last October, look no farther than the Federal Reserve."

BULL! As the Dow nears 7,500 in July 2002, Kudlow writes, "For those of you who have faith, now's the time to rely on it. Faith defeats the forces of darkness. Faith brings on the forces of good." Like so many celebrities facing the end of their run, Kudlow sounds destined to open a ministry.

⇥ **BOTTOM LINE** ⇤

The Internet economy has passed on, but Kudlow remains omnipresent.

JOHN SCHREIBER
Assistant Manager, Janus Fund

The logic behind the [AOL Time Warner] merger is impeccable. The combination of the two companies will create a media powerhouse the likes of which the world has never seen.

—Boston Globe,
February 28, 2000

AFTERMATH: As advertising slows and investors lose faith in the new paradigm, AOL Time Warner stock drifts down from $60 to $12.

OCTOBER 2000: "We don't think AOL Time Warner is vulnerable in any way."

BULL! Schreiber castigates naysayers as "uneducated institutional money fleeing both the Time Warner and AOL sides because they couldn't figure out how to value the company."

STRATEGY TO COMBAT DOWNTURN: In late 2002, the *New York Times* reports that "Janus has been reducing its exposure to once highflying stocks like AOL Time Warner."

BONUS FACT: In December 2001, Schreiber and CNBC's Maria Bartiromo discuss his disappointment with Jeff Skilling and Enron, one of Janus's 2001 top five holdings. When she asks him what stock he likes now, he offers up Enzon. It isn't a joke. (For the record, over the next year Enzon falls from $59 to $16.)

⇒ **BOTTOM LINE** ⇒
Educated institutional money fleeing a
media powerhouse the likes of which the world has never seen.

JEAN MONTY

CEO and Chairman, BCE

CP Photo Archive: Chuck Mitchell

The acquisition of Teleglobe will propel BCE into the global arena and greatly expand our opportunities for growth.

—The National Post, *February 29, 2000*

AFTERMATH: Over the next three years, the long-distance carrier Teleglobe racks up $3 billion in debt but no profits. In April 2002, BCE abandons Teleglobe and its debt, sending the company into bankruptcy. In September, Teleglobe announces the sale of its fiber-optic networks.

STRATEGY TO COMBAT DOWNTURN: Resignation. "It's obvious that BCE has gone through a difficult period with Teleglobe and I think it's important that we turn the page, in all respects. This morning we're looking forward, not backwards, at BCE." That will be great consolation to Teleglobe's creditors.

BULL! Teleglobe is just one of several costly dalliances—ExpressVu, Emergis, Sympatico, Globemedia, and BCI—that take BCE away from its core phone business. BCE stock rises 20 percent on news of Monty's resignation.

ALAN HOFFMAN

Senior Portfolio Manager, Value Line Asset Management

Tyco

The stock [Tyco] got knocked down a little bit over concern about accounting issues which we don't think is a real deal breaker. . . . We like the stock a lot and I would stay with it.

—*CNNfn*, Talking Stocks, *March 2, 2000*

AFTERMATH: The people unconcerned about accounting issues boost Tyco stock from $40 to $60. Then the concerned take it down to single digits.

BULL! Asked on the same show if he thinks Global Crossing is having difficulties, Hoffman responds: "I do not know the stock well, but I do know that they participate in what is going on in the whole telecommunications industry now in terms of consolidation. I think that they're well-positioned to prosper in that kind of environment. . . . I think they will probably do well in a consolidating industry." He likely knows the stock quite well now.

ANYTHING ABOUT WORLDCOM? "We like the long-distance business in general, just because, you know, that part of communications, including both voice and data transmissions, is a growing field."

There's no accounting for Hoffman.

ALAN HOFFMAN

Senior Portfolio Manager, Value Line Asset Management

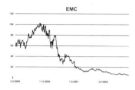

In terms of tech stocks to get into, I'm also in big favor of what we call the blue-chip tech: the Cisco Systems, the EMC, the IBM, the Dell.

—*CNNfn*, Market Coverage, *March 2, 2000*

AFTERMATH: The Cisco is $66 that day. By year end it's $38, en route to single digits. The EMC and the Dell go briefly higher before similarly collapsing. The IBM does slightly better but is also down by year end. More than two years later, the downtrends continue.

CAVEAT: Certainly there is a chance for investors to book a quick profit on the immediate upticks, but that isn't the mentality of the time, and certainly not the mentality of the Hoff, because his fund posts a return of –2.45 percent for the five years beginning in August 1997.

BULL! Hoffman is still upbeat at the end of 2001, predicting a 10 to 15 percent market return for 2002 and a Dow test of its high of 11,750: "I think we are going to experience a good year, not a great year."

CAPITULATION: July 20, 2002: "No matter what I think the market goes down. It's god-awful psychological black death out there. I don't have any projections or investment advice."

Okay, everybody give Mr. Hoffman a little space.

GREGG HYMOWITZ
Principal, Entrust Capital

Nasdaq Composite

2000 and beyond . . . equity markets soar.

—*CNN*, Moneyweek, December 18, 1999

AFTERMATH: Hymowitz falls back on an impressively thorough catalog of stock promoter clichés: technology stocks will not be fazed by interest rate hikes, companies without an Internet strategy are dead in the water, growth should be measured by revenue and not earnings, stocks of companies with "real businesses" always come back (particularly if they're big), stocks will go up because earnings comparisons will get easier, history implores us to stay in the market, and you're in for the long term so hang in there.

BULL! The Entrust Capital web site brags, "He appears regularly on CNBC's *Squawk Box* and *Business Center*, CNN's *Moneyline*, Fox News, and Bloomberg television." Which raises an obvious question: Is Gregg Hymowitz his real name or just a show business name?

⊰⊱ **BOTTOM LINE** ⊰⊱
Two unfortunate omissions from his cliché catalog: The trend is your friend and don't catch a falling knife.

GREGG HYMOWITZ

Principal, Entrust Capital

Aspect Communications

I really don't think valuation is all that relevant here . . . so I would stick with the market leaders.

—*CNNfn*, Market Coverage, *March 6, 2000*

AFTERMATH: Valuations become relevant a few days later when the NASDAQ peaks at 5,132 and then crumbles.

BULL! Hymowitz crows that he picked up most of his soaring stocks when they were cheap. His example? He bought Aspect Communications at $12 and in March 2000 it's $60. And it's "dominating its space," so he's adding to his holdings. Long story short: The company didn't make money then, doesn't make money now, and in 2002 you could get the shares for about a buck.

THE HITS KEEP COMIN': In the same show, he also recommends SBS Broadcasting on the basis of their Internet ventures. A couple of years later, that's down 80 percent. His other pick, Citigroup, is only down 20 percent.

BONUS FACT: When looking up Aspect Communications, we noticed there's also a NASDAQ-listed company called Aspect Medical Systems, which has a virtually identical price chart (about $60 to $2 in two years). You have to wonder if people were so reckless in the mania that they threw money at the wrong company.

⇥ **BOTTOM LINE** ⇤

That quote could've been the title of this book.

MONA ERAIBA
Semiconductor Analyst, Gruntal & Co.

Philadelphia Semiconductor Index

Actually, I think [the chip sector is] going to accelerate over the next year or so. Next two years I think we're going to continue to see very strong demand.

—*CNNfn*, Ahead of the Curve, *March 6, 2000*

AFTERMATH: SOXX, the Philadelphia Semiconductor Index, peaks at 1,346 the week of Eraiba's prediction. A series of earnings warnings later in the year takes it to 576.

STRATEGY TO COMBAT DOWNTURN: Denial. In July, one of her favorites, LSI Logic, delivers an earnings warning that sends the SOXX tumbling. Eraiba dismisses it as "a classic investor reaction. When you have a disappointment in one company, it's generalized, and the whole sector goes down." In October, with the SOXX down 35 percent from its peak, she claims, "Well, actually, the semiconductor industry is not doing so poorly."

BULL! On Valentine's Day of 2001, her love affair with the sector continues: "My sense: most of the decline is behind the industry, from a point of view of stocks. . . . I think all the stocks are now value stocks." Turns out, there is a little more decline left: 60 percent. A common lament in the earnings reports: "Revenues reflect decreased demand for products . . ."

≒ **BOTTOM LINE** ≒

If her specialty was anything other than analyzing semiconductor stocks, it really wouldn't look so bad.

MONA ERAIBA
Semiconductor Analyst, Gruntal & Co.

I would buy Intel. . . . It is a very cheap stock at current levels, even companies like Motorola, even though they have very specific problems, LSI Logic is interesting.

—*CNNfn*, Ahead of the Curve, *December 11, 2000*

AFTERMATH: None of the stocks are higher in six months, with Intel and Motorola both more than 15 percent lower. Within two years, all will be at least 50 percent lower.

THE HITS KEEP COMIN': A few months earlier, she gives her blessing to Texas Instruments, largely on the grounds that the cellular phone market would be "exceptionally strong" in 2001. Texas Instruments goes down about 14 percent in six months and, like the others, is eventually slashed in half.

BULL! In mid-2000, Eraiba is listed as the number-one televised stock picker in America by validea.com. In 2002, her name no longer appears among that site's leading forecasters. In fact, it doesn't really appear anywhere, as her national TV appearances have been dramatically curtailed since she rode the same stocks up and down the mountain.

⇥ **BOTTOM LINE** ⇤
Vanilla Ice was also number one for a few weeks.

CHRISTINE ROMANS
Reporter, CNNfn

Dow Jones Industrial Average

Come on, folks, they [tech stocks] don't just go straight up.

—*CNNfn*, Ahead of the Curve, *March 31, 2000*

AFTERMATH: The NASDAQ, which had gone from 5,047 to 4,457 in March 2000, goes to 3,265 within two weeks of Romans's pep talk and loses another thousand points by December. The worst part: Investors had to get up at 5:00 A.M. to hear this wisdom.

HAPPY TALK: Romans's exhortation not to panic is a response to this classic from the anchor David Haffenreffer: "And with every passing day, it looks like we're seeing more and more bargains in the high-tech sector as well." Again, this is on March 31, 2000. Is there a worse moment in market history to be spreading that message?

BULL! The above commercials for stock buying are especially interesting because they come not from brokerages or CEOs, who have a more obvious agenda, but from supposedly neutral newspeople. CNNfn doesn't get the criticism that CNBC does, though, because who's even heard of it? The people who proofread this book thought we just made up CNNfn in order to create dumb quotes.

⇒ **BOTTOM LINE** ⇐
Friends, Romans, anchormen, get it in gear!

MYRON KANDEL
Financial Editor and Anchor, CNNfn/Cofounder, CNN

Nasdaq Composite

Jan, the bottom line is, before the end of the year, the NASDAQ and Dow will be at new record highs.

—CNN, Street Sweep, April 4, 2000

AFTERMATH: The NASDAQ finishes the year down 40 percent from its high, the Dow 8 percent. On a historical note, Kandel's comment turns out to be the last-ever stock market commentary that mentions the NASDAQ first.

HITS KEEP ON COMIN´: On September 2, 2000, Kandel tells the CNN audience: "I think the Dow is going to hit a new record 12,000 before Election Day." As the Dow closes the year below 11,000, CNN anchor Stuart Varney begins to refer to Kandel as "Mr. Dow 12,000."

BULL! With almost no time left in 2000 to come up with another bad prediction, Kandel's year-end column on CNN.com delivers this buzzer beater: "I am sticking to my view that most—though not all—of the recent weakness was due to the presidential election mess. . . . When the presidential outcome is decided, the stock market will stage a solid rally." Sorry.

THE BEST-SELLER: In 1982, Kandel authored *How to Cash in on the Coming Stock Market Boom*, which foresaw the massive bull market. Don't forget to pick up his new book: *How to Push Your Luck.*

⇥ **BOTTOM LINE** ⇤

Jan, the bottom line is, before the end of the year,
Myron Kandel will shoot off his mouth again.

LLOYD D. WARD

CEO, iMotors

CP Photo Archive: Rodney White

I think iMotors will be a Fortune 500 company.

—New York Times, *February 7, 2001*

AFTERMATH: Just one month later, iMotors runs out of gas with reports that they'd used up $140 million in cash. Three months later the whole Internet engine seizes.

BULL! After iMotors, Ward tells the *New York Times*: "I'm clearly an NBA player and this was a pickup game. . . . I'm going to look around, but I don't know what I'm going to do next."

STRATEGY TO COMBAT DOWNTURN: Go to the government. Ward is now the CEO of the U.S. Olympic Committee.

BONUS QUOTE: "I always had this vision, this dream of being significant. I used to spend a lot of time talking about it then because I didn't have any view of CEO or president. It was just the high lama, big cheese, boss man."

＊ **BOTTOM LINE** ＊
Big cheese. Boss man. Bad timing.

PATRICIA CHADWICK

President, Ravengate Partners

Has it [QQQ] been volatile? Absolutely. Has it given up 90 percent the way some of the dot-com companies have? No, and it won't because those companies for the most part are real and have real earnings.

—*CNNfn*, Ahead of the Curve, *April 20, 2000*

AFTERMATH: Is she clueless? Pretty much. By late 2002, the QQQ (NASDAQ 100 shares) has lost 82 percent of its peak value. Almost half the companies on the index have no earnings. The rest have mostly scant earnings rendered suspect by a lack of options accounting.

BULL! On buying tech in 1999: "I think it's essential that you participate." In early 2000: "Well, I do think you have to have a big piece of your portfolio in technology." In late 2000: "This stock market has had a huge correction . . . and I think you can definitely nibble." So before the correction, big piece. After the correction, nibble.

BONUS PREDICTION: "Definitely not a recession." A few weeks later, the recession is officially under way.

⇒ **BOTTOM LINE** ⇒
When Chadwick says, "Avoid tech at all costs,"
the turnaround will be at hand.

PATRICIA CHADWICK

President, Ravengate Partners

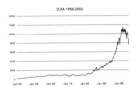

I think that we are writing a new book economically, and I think that happens every so often, and I think it happened a hundred years ago with the, you know, advent of the automobile and the real impact of the Industrial Revolution.

—*CNNfn*, Moneyline, *February 23, 2000*

AFTERMATH: Stock market crashes, just like at the end of the automobile-inspired boom of the '20s. Funny how the stock market shills-turned-historians pick out only the part of the story that supports their interests. Nothing new about this book.

BULL! Chadwick gets full points for originality, though, with this early 2000 answer to the question of whether higher interest rates could hurt business demand for her beloved tech giants: "I don't think so. . . . If anything they will do more to spend to offset the cost of interest rates going up. I think a lot of companies now just look at interest rates as one more cost of doing business. And if interest rates are going up, they say, Boy, I better get costs out of somewhere else, which drives them to spend." If anyone, anywhere knows what that could possibly mean, please contact us through the publisher.

Close the book on Chadwick.

TISH WILLIAMS

Columnist, UpsideToday

Ebbers is a master in the cutthroat tele-com market, where his main competitors are monopoly-fattened profit machines.

—Upside, *February 1997*

AFTERMATH: Tish Williams gets a regular spot writing for TheStreet.com. We're assuming that she's really cute.

BULL! Williams doesn't even pretend to be a journalist. She seems to be some kind of romance writer. What else would you call this? "Dear Larry [Ellison], . . . When the winds whipped at my back, as I shouted for mercy from the heavens in the Oracle parking lot, it was you I wanted. You I yearned for. You were all I could see."

BONUS QUOTE: "[Bernie] Ebbers is the man who grabbed the telecommunications industry by the heels and shook it until all its change fell out on the carpet. . . . He's a keeper."

⇥ **BOTTOM LINE** ⇥
Wouldn't you just kill to invest in a monopoly-fattened profit machine right about now?

BERNARD EBBERS

CEO, WorldCom Inc.

CF Photo Archive: Rogelio Solis

By and large, the employee base should be stable.

—Financial Times, *October 2, 1997*

AFTERMATH: The employee base is annihilated. Among the workers shown to the door: CEO Bernard Ebbers. Over the years, Ebbers received glowing notices for increasing share price, and he doesn't disappoint even on his last day—his departure sends the stock up 15 percent.

REASON FOR RESIGNATION: "Bernie was increasingly frustrated," says new CEO John Sidgmore, April 30, 2002

BULL! Ebbers has changed jobs before. His credits include used car salesman, motel owner, high school basketball coach, milkman, and novelist. The last reveals a love of fiction that appears to extend to WorldCom's financial statements. In February 2002, Ebbers reassures investors in a conference call: "WorldCom has a solid base of bill-paying customers, strong fundamentals, a solid balance sheet, manageable leverage, and nearly $10 billion in available liquidity. Bankruptcy or a credit default is not a concern." Four months later, WorldCom declares bankruptcy. Maybe Ebbers's comments were misheard due to faulty phone lines.

⇒ **BOTTOM LINE** ⇒
Weak End at Bernie's

PHILIP ORLANDO

Chief Investment Officer, Value Line Management

Halliburton

It's a very attractive deal, done at a good price, which materially enhances the underlying value of Halliburton's shares. . . . Our analysis suggests that $65 to $70 per share in the near term would be a reasonable target.

—Oil & Gas Investor,
April 1998

AFTERMATH: As Dresser's asbestos-related claims add up, Halliburton falls 70 percent.

BULL! Why did no one, including analysts like Orlando, consider Dresser's asbestos claims a problem? In 1999, the *Boston Globe* quotes John Wall, a lawyer who represents dozens of laid-off employees: "[CEO Dick] Cheney would have had to know. That would be part of his due diligence. If he didn't know, that would be total incompetence."

BACK AND FORTH: According to the *New York Times*, "The two chief executives felt so comfortable with each other they decided this [due diligence] would not be necessary." The *Washington Post* pipes in with a Cheney spokesperson, who says that the merger, "like all major acquisitions, was subject to enormous due diligence by highly qualified subject matter experts," while Dresser President Donald Vaughn says it was "easier and shorter" than other mergers.

✦ **BOTTOM LINE** ✦
Cheney wants to take over Iraq.
Let's hope they don't have an asbestos problem.

DICK CHENEY

CEO, Halliburton

CP Photo Archive: Frank Gunn

The [Halliburton-Dresser] merger is designed to result in long-term benefits for the company's stakeholders— its customers, employees, and shareholders.

—*Halliburton press release, September 29, 1998*

AFTERMATH: Well, maybe not the employees. Or the shareholders. After the merger, Halliburton lays off over 11,000 employees— almost 11 percent of its workers. Then rising concerns over Dresser's asbestos liabilities hit the stock price, which drops from its 1997 peak of $60 to $14.

STRATEGY TO COMBAT DOWNTURN: Run for vice president. In a televised debate casually mention that "I've been out in the private sector building a business, hiring people, creating jobs."

BULL! Although even critics agree that part of Halliburton's problem is a lagging oil market, most recognize the merger as a disaster. Lester Brickman, professor and *defense* consultant for asbestos manufacturers, tells the *New York Times* that the merger was "a horrible mistake. No one could possibly argue otherwise." Nobody except Dick Cheney, who, at the time, calls it "one of the most exciting things I've been involved in."

BONUS QUOTE: "As we go into 2000, circumstances will be better than they were at the beginning of 1999."

⇥ **BOTTOM LINE** ⇤
Eighteen thousand jobs lost since 1999.

DICK CHENEY

CEO, Halliburton

Halliburton

I get good advice, if you will, from their [Arthur Andersen] people based upon how we're doing business and how we're operating, over and above the normal, by-the-book auditing arrangement.

—*Arthur Andersen video, 1996*

AFTERMATH: On July 15, 2002, the SEC announces that Halliburton "is under SEC scrutiny for the way it accounted for cost overruns on construction jobs during Mr. Cheney's tenure." In other words, they reported profits "above the normal, by-the-book auditing arrangement."

HIDE 'N' SEEK: Cheney becomes the Ninja of Washington, appearing suddenly and in silence. When he does talk, it's usually at obscure fundraisers, where he rarely takes questions. After months of questions he finally offers this niblet: "There are editorial writers all over America poised to put pen to paper and condemn me for exercising undue, improper influence if I say too much about it." Naturally, everyone prints that.

BULL! Cheney is MIA at any of the president's corporate crackdown speeches and the SEC investigation, which doesn't call him to testify.

꘎ **BOTTOM LINE** ꘎

Bush changes Cheney's nickname from Big Time to Possibility of Time.

HENRY BLODGET

King of the Internet/Analyst, Merrill Lynch

Getty Images: Jean-Christian Bourcart

InfoSpace is very much in a good position to benefit from the growth of wireless, which we think will be the big opportunity going forward. Here we have a one-year target of $100.

—*StockHouse.com,*
May 4, 2000

AFTERMATH: "Can we please reset this stupid price target and rip this piece of junk [InfoSpace] off whatever list it's on. If you have to downgrade it, downgrade it."

BULL! Dr. Debasis Kanjilal claims that he invested in InfoSpace on Blodget's recommend. He alleges losses of $518,000 and sues Merrill Lynch. New York Attorney General Eliot Spitzer uncovers e-mail calling stocks "dogs" despite "buy" ratings. Merrill Lynch pays $400,000 to Kanjilal and settles with the state of New York out of court, paying a $100 million fine. They also apologize. Sort of. Merrill Lynch "regrets that there were instances in which certain of our Internet sector research analysts expressed views which at certain points may have appeared inconsistent with Merrill Lynch's published recommendations." Huh? They regret getting caught?

FUTURE PLANS: "I kind of felt it was time for the next chapter, and Merrill made it easy to do that." Blodget also cites wanting to spend more time with his wife and to finish a book on, what else, the Internet. Mary Meeker is expected to recommend.

DAVID KOMANSKY

Chairman and CEO, Merrill Lynch

There is no basis for the allegations made today by the New York Attorney General. His conclusions are just plain wrong.

—*Merrill Lynch press release, April 8, 2002*

AFTERMATH: On May 21, Merrill Lynch reaches a deal with the New York attorney general. The release reads, "Messrs. Komansky and O'Neal noted that the company was 'pleased to put this matter behind us in a way that seriously addresses investor concerns. We believe strongly in the integrity of our research, which has served investors well for many decades. At the same time we have apologized for any unprofessional behavior.'"

BULL! "The [$100 million] settlement represents neither evidence nor admission of wrongdoing or liability."

WORDS TO LIVE BY: "I think the result of all these changes that are being implemented is that CEOs will be far more at risk than they've ever been before. I think that's appropriate, and I don't think it's a problem." Komansky, one of the most respected men on Wall Street, knew of what he spoke. Two weeks previous to making this statement, he announced that he'd be retiring a year early.

Leave by the back door, please.

HARVEY L. PITT

Chairman, Securities Exchange Commission

CP Photo Archive: Dennis Cook

When I turned in my private practitioner's hat and took on the position of the chairmanship, I took on the representation of individual stock owners.

—SEC's investor summit, May 10, 2002

AFTERMATH: The individual stockholders he's referring to are likely Skilling and Lay, as Pitt did nothing but wax on about the need for partnership between the public and private sectors. Meanwhile, the always eager New York attorney general, Eliot Spitzer, breaks out the handcuffs and gets Merrill to agree to base analysts' pay on accuracy and not on pumping stocks of Merrill clients. Then he fines them, tries to separate research and investment, all while finding the time to shave.

BULL! Pitt further enrages the public when Congress asks for the SEC's suggestions regarding corporate responsibility legislation. He includes a request for a raise and a change in position that would put him alongside Colin Powell and John Ashcroft in the cabinet. Ignoring calls for his resignation (maybe he couldn't hear them through all the laughter) Pitt then fails to inform fellow SEC commissioners and the White House that the incoming accounting oversight board chief, William Webster, is the former head of an audit committee at a small firm accused of fraud. Pitt says, "It would not pose a problem." He resigns on the night of midterm elections when the cameras are otherwise occupied.

⇌ **BOTTOM LINE** ⇌

Pitt's private practitioner's hat: Accounting industry lobbyist.

DONALD LAMBRO

Columnist, Washington Times

Nasdaq Composite

The gloom that has permeated the stock market for the past few months can be traced directly to Al Gore's anti-business, pro-regulatory, tax-and-spend campaign . . . the deepening weakness in the financial markets, especially the technology sector, closely paralleled Mr. Gore's earlier rise in the polls.

—Washington Times,
October 12, 2000

AFTERMATH: The NASDAQ is sliced in half in the first eighteen months of the Bush administration, despite an aggressive rate cut campaign by the Federal Reserve.

PAINTED INTO A CORNER: Having blamed a nonpolitical event on politics, Lambro and other conservatives are stuck trying to explain why Bush's pro-business administration is presiding over a plunging market. Their favorite angle: The market collapse was caused by immoral acts in corporate America, and all immoral behavior in America can be traced to Bill Clinton.

BULL! Lambro comes up with a new stock market theory on November 29, 2001: "A clear and decisive victory in Afghanistan . . . would send the stock market soaring, giving a new and welcome meaning to the term 'wealth effect.'" The clear and decisive victory happens, and the markets keep tanking.

⇥ **BOTTOM LINE** ⇤

This guy's talent is wasted in journalism.
He's got the forecasting skills to be an analyst.

LAWRENCE LINDSEY

Bush Chief Economic Adviser

Associated Press: Ben Margot

Let's face it, Mr. Gore has a basically anti-business agenda. When he began his populist tour after the convention and went on his attack on business, that's when the markets started down.

—Washington Times, October 12, 2000

AFTERMATH: Gore and his agenda are vanquished. It becomes safe again for business to continue the innovation and productivity that have provided America's great prosperity. The markets keep diving.

EXPLANATION: When no "Bush rally" materializes after the election is decided, Charles Pradilla of SG Cowen Securities sums it up best: "You could've elected Pat Buchanan or Moses, it wouldn't have mattered. NASDAQ is working out its problems with valuations and earnings disappointments."

BULL! Lindsey changes his tune during the Dubya presidency, blaming the market decline on the "hangover" from the stock market bubble. It is a familiar tune, because he sang it loudly back in the mid-'90s, when he was the first on the Federal Reserve Board to recognize the bubble and urge Greenspan to action. "Readers of this transcript five years from now can check this fearless predictioin: Profits will fall short of expectation."

⟱ BOTTOM LINE ⟱
Lindsey can plead "temporary stupidity," also known as "campaigning."

69

GEORGE W. BUSH
President/MBA

CP Photo Archive: Ryan Remiorz

There is a fundamental difference between my opponent and me. He trusts only government to manage our retirement. I trust individual Americans to make their own decisions and manage their own money.

—*Speech, Rancho Cucamonga California, May 15, 2000*

AFTERMATH: Apparently Bush isn't talking about his mother-in-law, a retired book-keeper and individual American, who the previous September bought 200 shares of Enron at $40.90. Enron peaks at $90 a share in late 2000 but, following the buy-and-hold strategy wafting from the airwaves, Ms. Jenna Welch stays the course until December 4, 2001, at $0.42. Total loss? $8,094. At Enron alone, 4,000 people lose their jobs and their life savings, not only because the company would not let them touch their 401(k)s but also because they unwisely chose to invest heavily in one stock.

STRATEGY: Create new laws that address corporate responsibility but that, unfortunately, cannot address the long history of human greed and stupidity. Then try to convince people to buy: "If they buy stock, they're buying value—as opposed to buying . . . into a bubble."

BULL! According to *Time*, Americans responded to the call to invest in 2001 and sank a record $140 billion in their 401(k) balances, which promptly shrank by 4 percent. "Ninety-five percent of people ages fifty-five to sixty-four and still working plan to get another job after they retire."

━ **BOTTOM LINE** ━
Bush's plan screeched to a halt along with the Enron jet.

THOMAS WHITE

Chairman and CEO, Enron Ventures Corp.

The central thrust of Enron's vision is the creation of clean energy solutions.

—*Enron press release, December 9, 1997*

AFTERMATH: In 1998, White is named vice chairman of Enron Energy Services the same day Andrew Fastow makes CFO. In 2001, Bush names White secretary of the army. Eight months later White adds himself to his list of things to defend as Enron's central vision is revealed to be cooking books.

BULL! Before the scandal, White continues with his corporate cred theme: "We effectively are the CEOs of wholly owned subsidiaries of the Department of Defense." As corporate leaders are pilloried, Washington chucks the CEO bit. White denies charges of market manipulation to the Senate Committee: "I am responsible as an officer of the company for the portion of that company that I ran. . . . The deals that we put together, within the accounting structure that was the standard in the industry, I stand behind."

BONUS QUOTE: "I took straight over the cliff, along with thousands of other investors." He fails to add "I resign."

⇥ **BOTTOM LINE** ⇤

White stands behind while America bends over.

PHIL GRAMM

Senator (R–TX)

CP Photo Archive: Bill Janscha

We have learned that we promote economic growth, and we promote stability, by having competition and freedom. I am proud to be here because this is an important bill. It is a deregulatory bill. I believe that that is the wave of the future.

—Senate Banking Committee press release, November 12, 1999

AFTERMATH: Gramm's favorite—deregulation—takes a hit when it is revealed that Enron made billions from brownouts. What surprises most people is that Enron made any money at all from energy.

SURPRISE! In 1993 his wife, Wendy, chair of the Commodity Futures Trading Commission, exempted energy trading from regulation. Then she took a job on Enron's board of directors and audit committee. In all, she was reportedly paid between $915,000 and $1,850,000 in stocks, dividends, and salary. Oh, and let's not forget the $176,000 attendance fees. Attendance fees? What is that? For showing up?

BULL! Surprisingly or not surprisingly, depending on your level of cynicism, the Senate investigation does not call the senator's wife. The Gramms cry that they lost 600 Gs in Enron, which isn't so bad when you consider the $260,000 in campaign contributions.

REASON FOR RESIGNATION: After "a long and difficult period of soul searching," and two months before the Enron investigation goes public, Gramm announces his retirement. Then he accepts a job at—don't laugh—a Swiss bank, which owned significant Enron debt and "bought Enron's trading operation."

⇥ **BOTTOM LINE** ⇤

What have we learned here, Senator?

LAWRENCE SUMMERS

Clinton Treasury Secretary

CP Photo Archive: David Guttenfelder

With this bill, the American financial system takes a major step forward toward the twenty-first century. One that will benefit American consumers, business and the national economy.

—Statement LS-241 on the repeal of the Glass-Steagall Act, Washington, November 12, 1999

AFTERMATH: Not two years after Clinton repealed the Glass-Steagall Act of 1933, the public cries foul when they discover that brokers and bankers are not only talking to each other but conspiring to mislead customers. As the year unfolds, consumers learn that investment banks are controlling their analysts' ratings and that investment clients are getting first crack at lucrative IPOs. Hell, they didn't skirt the Chinese Wall, they pulled the damned thing down.

RESULT: Research directors of fourteen Wall Street firms come up with guidelines to cover analyst pay, disclosure, and rebuilding the wall. All voluntary, of course.

BULL! The year 2002 marks the worst corporate scandals of the twenty-first century. Of course the century is only three years old, but it is still pretty ugly.

One step forward. Two steps back.

SANFORD WEILL

CEO, Citigroup

CP Photo Archive: Richard Drew

We think that what the customer has to pay today for the services that they get from a full service firm is really not very much, relative to the information that they get, how they are helped. So, we expect that business to continue to grow.

—Trading Places,
April 6, 1998

AFTERMATH: Citicorp and Travelers Group join to create a full-service financial service company just in time for Clinton to repeal the Glass-Steagall Act.

BULL! Travelers's holdings include the investment bank Salomon Smith Barney. As the market pulls away from Internet stocks, it appears that customers paying for their full service are helped as they bask in SSB's sunny ratings. And then there are the hot IPO offerings to Citigroup customers. Added value. And what about that sliding Enron debt that swept from balance sheet to balance sheet? Full service. And you don't pay much.

UNDER THE UMBRELLA: Citigroup: "Mr. Weill never told any analyst what to write, and any suggestion that he did is outrageous and untrue." Then a Grubman e-mail surfaces that alleges Grubman upped his AT&T rating in exchange for Weill's help in getting his twins into preschool. Grubman later denies the truth of his own e-mail while Weill admits he asked Grubman to take "a fresh look . . . in the light of the dramatic transformation" of AT&T. You decide.

✥ **BOTTOM LINE** ✥

Today Citigroup customers are paying for SEC investigations, civil lawsuits, and $200,000 a year to 92nd Street Y preschool.

ROBERT E. RUBIN

Clinton Treasury Secretary

CP Photo Archive: Dennis Cook

We believe financial service firms ought to be able to organize themselves in the way that they feel makes the most business sense, just as businesses do across our economy, and not in a government-dictated, one-size-fits-all structure.

—*Capitol Hill, June 17, 1998*

AFTERMATH: Rubin helps shape the Gramm-Leach-Bliley Act, which is driven by the Citicorp-Travelers merger.

CITICORP, APRIL 1998: "Citicorp and Travelers Group expect that current laws restricting bank holding companies from participating in insurance underwriting activities will change." As if by magic, they do.

CUT TO: July 4, 1999, Rubin resigns.

CUT TO: On October 29, 1999, Citigroup announces the appointment of Rubin to the office of chairman, making him number three in the chain of command.

BULL! The Gramm-Leach-Bliley Act, meant to update the changing banking sector, allows the Citigroup merger to go through. Citigroup, which owns SSB and which has its fingerprints on Enron and WorldCom banking, is currently under investigation and the subject of numerous lawsuits. This leads us to the trillion-dollar question: Can a "financial service" company fail? Are they too big to fail? Who bails them out?

⇥ **BOTTOM LINE** ⇥
You do.

JACK GRUBMAN

Analyst, Salomon Smith Barney/Pied Piper of Telecom

CP Photo Archive: Kenneth Lambert

What used to be a conflict is now a synergy. Someone like me who is banking intensive would have been looked at disdainfully by the buy side fifteen years ago. Now they know that I'm in the flow of what's going on.

—Business Week, *May 15, 2000*

AFTERMATH: Grubman is in the flow of what's going on, but not in the way he planned. With news of NASD, SEC, and Eliot Spitzer investigations and forty investor lawsuits, he becomes the poster boy of tainted analysts.

STRATEGY TO COMBAT DOWNTURN: Keep screaming "Buy" until you're drowned out by the chorus screaming "Resign."

REASON FOR RESIGNATION: "The relentless series of negative statements about my work, all of which I believe unfairly single me out, has begun to undermine my efforts to analyze telecommunications companies."

BULL! Grubman didn't mind being singled out when things were good: "I'm sculpting the industry. I get feedback from institutions and CEOs. It feeds on itself. It's a virtuous circle." That's hard to read.

BONUS FACT: Fat cat can't even tell the truth in his own bio. Said he graduated from MIT. Reality: Boston U.

BONUS FACT: NASD fined Grubman $15 million, less than half of his reported severance.

⇒ **BOTTOM LINE** ⇒
Back to disdainful looks.

JACK GRUBMAN
Analyst, Salomon Smith Barney/Pied Piper of Telecom

WorldCom is the one I would buy because it has the least execution risk to get back going, the best set of assets, the best revenue mix, and the best balance sheet of the three [WorldCom, Sprint, AT&T].

—Fortune,
December 18, 2000

AFTERMATH: Analysts abandon WCOM over the next two years, but Grubman maintains his buy. WorldCom restates earnings, sheds itself of executives, who are subsequently arrested, and is delisted by NASDAQ. Grubman moves from his December buy ($14.93) to an April neutral ($4.01) and finally downgrades to underperform in June ($0.91). In August ($0.12), Grubman quits.

ANALYST OR BROKER? Some media do criticize Grubman's cozy relationship with bankers and CEOs, but it takes the biggest bankruptcy in America to catch the public's, the watchdogs', and Congress's attention. Grubman's other favorites? Winstar, Global Crossing, Metromedia Fiber Network, McLeod USA, Rhythms NetConnections, to name a few. All buys. All bankrupt. All underwritten by Salomon Smith Barney.

BULL! Grubman was open about his relationship with companies. He went to board meetings, attended Ebbers's wedding, and sneered at objectivity: "The other word for it is uninformed." According to the *New York Post* he even expensed his trip to Ebbers's wedding. Stamped on the top left corner? IBD. Investment Banking Department.

⇥ **BOTTOM LINE** ⇥
Banned from the securities industry for life.

TATSUYUKI SAEKI

CEO, NASDAQ Japan

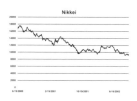

Nikkei

This is an important day for Japanese investors and in the history of Japan's financial markets. . . . It is truly a new day for the Japanese economy.

—*Press release on NASDAQ Japan's launch, June 19, 2000*

AFTERMATH: NASDAQ Japan shuts its doors in August 2002 due to "economic and market conditions."

BULL! As the struggling Japanese economy turns ugly in 2001, Saeki unloads on the Japanese government for tax regulations that penalize workers who switch companies: "Japan is more communist than China." NASDAQ Chief Hardwick Simmons says the answer is for Japanese people to start buying tech stocks instead of saving.

STRATEGY TO COMBAT DOWNTURN: Saeki falls on the sword in May 2002, after NASDAQ Japan fails to secure a key strategic alliance.

⇥ **BOTTOM LINE** ⇤
Kamikaze mission.

JEAN-MARIE MESSIER

Chairman and CEO, Vivendi Universal

CP Photo Archive: Michel Lupchitz

If the Bronfman family accepts Vivendi's offer, it is because they really believe that Vivendi is capable of creating a lot of value in the coming years—and they are right to do so.

—Newsday, *June 20, 2000*

AFTERMATH: Regardless of what the Bronfman family thinks, the merger stinks. In 2001, Vivendi, formerly a water and sewage company, offers up France's largest corporate loss—ever. By 2002, Vivendi starts to sell off its recently acquired $70 billion assets, its stock sits in the dumper, and Messier is ousted in a hysterical corporate stare down that he maintains is rigged.

BULL! Poor Universal—first bought by a Canadian booze family and then sold to a French water company. Who can make music and movies under those conditions? As for Canal Plus, another Messier acquisition, riots break out in France when he fires an underperforming but popular station head. French people—they even take television seriously. Vivendi shares drop over 70 percent in 2002.

THE AUTOBIOGRAPHY: *J6M.com*, which reportedly stands for "Jean-Marie Messier: Moi-Même, Maître du Monde."

TRANSLATION: Jean-Marie Messier: Myself, Master of the World.

≒ **BOTTOM LINE** ≒

James Cameron, move over. There's a new pompous ass in town.

79

JEAN-MARIE MESSIER

Chairman and CEO, Vivendi Universal

Vivendi Universal

By offering our customers an exclusive opportunity to listen to the new song by Celine Dion . . . on the one hand we can boost Universal Music, but also the usage and loyalty of customers [to Vivendi's Internet portal].

—press conference to announce merger, June 22, 2000

AFTERMATH: Messier is quickly informed by his fellow executive Edgar Bronfman that Celine Dion is not on the Universal label. In fairness, it's hard to keep track of such a wide variety of subsidiaries let alone merge them efficiently, one big reason the media convergence strategy unravels and Messier is fired.

BULL! After the merger of Universal and Vivendi, Messier beams. "For the first time in Europe, there is a communication group of a size that will be able to rival all the American giants." It certainly ends up rivaling AOL.

BRIGHT SIDE: Messier, who loves America so much he moved his primary residence there to the disgust of the easily disgusted French, wins a coveted American honor: His dismissal in July 2002 makes him *Time*'s Person of the Week.

RICHARD MCGINN

CEO, Lucent Technologies

Lucent Technologies

Nokia had a miss a couple of years ago and has come back strong. Nortel had a down period. . . . We will be the leader. We are regaining momentum.

—Business Week,
June 26, 2000

AFTERMATH: Lucent stock begins its descent from its $84 high and lands below $20. Lucent fires McGinn in December 2000. Then they fire 49,000 other people. Nothing helps. Lucent eventually sells for the price of a ten-minute long-distance call.

BULL! Lucent gives McGinn a $12.5 million settlement and, hold your breath, an annual pension of $870,000. If Lucent had run the Revolution, they would have given Benedict Arnold a bonus.

BONUS QUOTE: "For the foreseeable future, what matters is the condition of the balance sheet, the ability to demonstrate a plan for free cash flow. Nothing exotic. Everything transparent."

BULL! Named one of *Business Week*'s 1999 Top 25 Executives.

Momentum goes both ways, but McGinn gets his pension every year.

TUCKER CARLSON

Host, CNN, Crossfire

They [Bush-Cheney campaign] have been flirting around with this dumb stock-option business, and otherwise wasting time.

—Weekly Standard,
August 2000

AFTERMATH: Forget you ever said that.

BULL! In a July 2002 interview with Ralph Nader, Carlson blames the shareholders: "I've always wondered this, Where were investors, say, when a corporation or a company that was, in fact, losing money was paying himself $10 million a year, presumably they have some role, some say in his compensation." Has this guy ever owned stock? As the scandals intensify, so does Carlson's tone. In September he refers to Cisco's accounting as "corporate malfeasance" and says, "Cisco Systems reported income of $4.6 billion. It turns out they didn't take into account a lot of things, including stock options. Had it been adjusted, it would have been $2.74 billion. Almost $2 billion, looks like, they inflated their earnings."

Welcome to *Crossfire* . . . flirting with this dumb stock-option business.

CHARLES WANG

CEO, Computer Associates International

Computer Associates

For us to be successful, we have to make you successful and . . . we are absolutely committed to that process.

—Infoworld Daily News, *April 27, 1998*

AFTERMATH: It's hard to get rich when your stock is dropping from the $50 range to $8. Unless you're the CEO.

BONUS BONUS: In 1999, shareholders support Wang and vote against limiting the 1998 $1.1 billion bonus in stock for three executives including Wang, who is in for two thirds of the shares. After the vote, he tells *Newsday*, "I think the vote speaks for itself." The company takes a one-time write-down of $1.07 billion to accommodate the executives, despite soft sales. The stock loses 31 percent on the announcement.

BULL! Shareholder Lisa Sanders disagrees and takes CA to court. She wins. The judge rules that, despite stock splits, CA's directors did not have authority to issue an extra 9.5 million shares above and beyond what the shareholders approved in 1995. The execs, including Wang, are ordered to repay approximately $550 million in shares.

⇥ **BOTTOM LINE** ⇤
With success comes litigation.

JAMES CRAMER

Host, *CNBC*, Kudlow and Cramer/*Author*, You Got Screwed

CBS Marketwatch tried to drive our stock down as low as possible and buy us. . . . There are a series of things a company can do to manipulate a stock down. Why don't you ask them?

—Business Week, *March 6, 2000*

AFTERMATH: Shares of TheStreet.com fall from $12 to below $1, because one sure way to manipulate a stock down is to lose money in every year of operation. CBS MarketWatch follows the same profitless path into the stock price abyss.

BULL! Cramer is very familiar with the manipulation issue, having endured a suspension from CNBC in 1998 after denigrating a stock that he allegedly had planned to short. He'd also clashed with colleagues at Fox News for allegedly promoting TheStreet.com stock on the air. He subsequently writes a column accusing *Bull!* favorite Gregg Hymowitz of irresponsibly moving a stock on CNBC and calling for a halt to discussion of small-cap stocks on national television. Also in that column, he implies he may have been singled out for suspension because his web site competes with CNBC.com.

BONUS QUOTE: February 10, 2000: "Enron is certainly for real."

~≈ **BOTTOM LINE** ≈~

Business Week's Marcia Vickers said it best: "Hell hath no fury like a talking head/financial columnist/money manager whose stock is in the tank."

ERIK GUSTAFSON

Growth Fund Manager, Stein Roe & Farnham

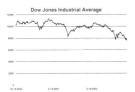

Dow Jones Industrial Average

This morning had all the characteristics of a capitulation sell. There was true fear in the market—it was palpable. There has been a lot of damage to this market, and I think it's just about finished.

—Chicago Tribune,
October 19, 2000

AFTERMATH: Many more "capitulations," and much more use of the word *capitulation*, which takes its place alongside *hanging chad* as one of the most overused expressions of the millennium.

STUPIDITY SEQUEL: On July 2, 2001, Gustafson tells CNN's Lou Dobbs, "There really hasn't been a lot of shelter in this bear market storm we've seen for fifteen months. I think we're just about through. . . . I think we have put in a bottom in the April lows." The annoying thing about most sequels is they're just rehashes of the originals.

ANOTHER GEM: On June 18, 2002, he says, "We're laying the groundwork for a rally." For the next month, the Dow goes virtually straight down by a spectacular 20 percent.

BULL! In 1999, CNN says Gustafson manages "$4 billion in assets." In 2002, *Bloomberg News* says he "runs a $1.2 billion Growth Stock Fund." That's what they call growth in the Bizarro World.

✦ **BOTTOM LINE** ✦

If Gustafson were reading this page, he would've predicted that
the four previous lines were the Bottom Line.

JON BURNHAM

Chairman and CEO, Burnham Securities

Siebel Systems

It's a company that couldn't be doing better. They [Siebel] don't have any significant competition, but it's selling at a very high price and I love the stock, long term. I'm not selling any.

— *CNNfn*, Talking Stocks, *October 30, 2000*

AFTERMATH: Well, we can't speak about Siebel Systems long term, but Jon Burnham can't shut up about it, so we'll let him talk. It's at $98 at the time of the interview.

BULL! In April 2001, Burnham tells CNNfn, "So far as I know, Siebel's business is excellent, and, if the market is going to hold this gain and go further over the next few months, I would say that Siebel has seen its low. I think so." It's at $45. By June, he's slightly more cautious. "I think Siebel is an attractive stock at this level, if you have a strong stomach." It's hitting $40. In December, when the stock hits the mid-$20s, "Companies . . . will come back rather strongly, companies like Siebel Systems, which as you know, I've been following a long time." A month later, Burnham is back on CNNfn: "Siebel Systems is another company that clearly has turned around their business. They had a much better fourth quarter. They're going to have a much better year than most Wall Street firms are looking for. And I think it's an attractive time." In June, Siebel announces that its profits are down 61 percent from 2001. At time of printing Siebel is $5+.

Abused analyst syndrome.

LOUIS RUKEYSER

Host, *PBS*, Wall Street Week

CP Photo Archive: Lisa Helfert

[Market naysayers] always get a hearing because people are scared to death about money. . . . So one of these charlatans comes along and says, Oh, it's a lot worse than you think. People say, Oh, I'm finally hearing the real inside story. They've been the worst forecasters consistently for thirty years.

—*CNN*, Street Sweep, *November 3, 2000*

AFTERMATH: The real charlatans are revealed, and none of them are naysayers. They're CEOs who promised unattainable profits, auditors who gave those companies clean reports, and analysts who gave strong buy ratings to "dogs." Not to mention media cheerleaders who gave the mania their stamp of approval, or who shouted down any dissenters.

THE YAYSAYERS: CNBC, aka "Bubblevision" to naysayers, is widely considered the holy temple for those with blind faith in the stock market. So it stands to reason that Rukeyser would land there after getting dumped by PBS in 2002.

BULL! For his outstanding achievement in the field of telling people what they want to hear, Louis Rukeyser has received honorary doctorates from eight different universities. Strangely, he was not given honorary spots on the school cheerleading squads. Ah, wry wit worthy of Mr. Rukeyser himself. Drifting off yet?

⊱ **BOTTOM LINE** ⊰

The worst forecasters of the last thirty years may be the best ones
of the next thirty years.

LOUIS RUKEYSER

Host, PBS, Wall Street Week

S&P 500

When we started, the theory was that the little guy always got the short end of the stick, never had a chance. I think one of the things that we've helped demonstrate is that if the little guy, by which I mean male or female, small individual investor, shows common sense, not only can he or she compete with the institutions, it can beat them.

—*CNN, Street Sweep, November 3, 2000*

AFTERMATH: While the Ken Lays and Gary Winnicks are quietly selling their stocks at the peak, individual investors who may be leaning in that direction are discouraged by media stars like Rukeyser, who repeatedly assure them that the stock market is the place to be.

BULL! And the beat goes on. As the market takes yet another plunge in June 2002, Rukeyser tells Katie Couric: "I would remind folks that the winning formula is buy low, sell high. Not panic and get out when prices are low." This is interesting, not only because then prices are anything but low from a historical perspective but also because he was not advocating selling when things were unquestionably high two years earlier.

ALL ABOARD: Rukeyser conducts a semiannual "Investment Cruise" in the Caribbean. If the boat ever starts sinking, watch for him to mock passengers who get in the lifeboats as "panicking."

✢ **BOTTOM LINE** ✣

Great news for this champion of the little guy:
Since 2000, the market has created a lot more little guys.

LOUIS RUKEYSER

Host, *PBS*, Wall Street Week

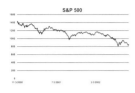

Oh, I think over the next year or two [the stock market] will be higher, and I know over the next five to ten years it will be higher.

—*CNN*, Street Sweep, *November 3, 2000*

AFTERMATH: Almost two years later, whichever stock market he may have had in mind is way, way down. Big cap (43 percent), small cap (41 percent), and tech (70 percent) all crater, despite this unqualified endorsement from one of Wall Street's august elders.

BULL! The markets are already down sharply from their highs when Rukeyser, who talks about championing the "little guy" investors, gives his flock the preceding reassurance. The message is classic mania mentality—keep on buying because stocks are not risky if you hold them for a few years.

REALITY: Stock markets go through long periods when they do not go up and can even go down. Americans learned this in the 1930s and '40s, and the Japanese Nikkei had zero return if you bought in 1983 and held for two decades. In defense of Rukeyser, he sits in a very comfortable chair and may have slept through both periods.

⇥ **BOTTOM LINE** ⇤
No wonder Rukeyser got kicked off PBS.
His viewers were too broke to make pledges.

89

JEFFREY SKILLING

President and CEO, Enron

CP Photo Archive: Kenneth Lambert

We have a better business model. It's a fundamentally better business model.

—Informationweek, *November 6, 2000*

AFTERMATH: Bankruptcy. Congressional hearings. Finger-pointing. SEC investigations. Arthur Andersen's collapse. Nightly photos of retirees heading back to the job boards. Corporate responsibility legislation. Shareholder lawsuits. Political fallout. Loss of faith in the markets. Loss of investors. Talk of double dip recession. Ball fields getting name changes. Universities changing chair names. Secondhand stores opening. Trash collection fees going up in Connecticut.

REASON FOR RESIGNATION: "I am resigning for personal reasons. I want to thank Ken Lay for his understanding of this purely personal decision."

BULL! 1996: Corporate Conscience Award for Environmental Stewardship

BULL! 1997: James H. McGraw Award for Business Excellence by *Electrical World*

BULL! 1999: Ranked 24 in 100 Best Companies to Work for in America by *Fortune*

BULL! 2000: Ranked 22 in 100 Best Companies to Work for in America by *Fortune*

✦ **BOTTOM LINE** ✦

$62 million in exercised options.

KENNETH LAY
Chairman, Enron

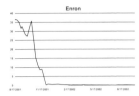

There are absolutely no problems that had anything to do with Jeff's departure. There are no accounting issues, no trading issues, no reserve issues, no previously unknown-problem issues. The company is probably in the strongest and best shape that it has ever been in.

—Business Week *Online, August 24, 2001*

AFTERMATH: Enron shares sink from their $90 high to $2 on eBay when Enron lays off over 4,000 employees and files for bankruptcy.

BULL! Meanwhile, back on the ranch, Lay quietly dumps $20 million worth of Enron stock while calming the employees. "I want to assure you that I have never felt better about the prospects for the company. Our performance has never been stronger; our business model has never been more robust; our growth has never been more certain." Then he bars employees from selling stock starting October 16, the day Enron announces a $618 million third-quarter loss and a $1.2 billion reduction in shareholder equity. During the lockdown, Enron's stock drops by almost a third. Lay's 2001 compensation: a tidy $247 million.

BONUS QUOTE: "You're going to do what?"—to Jeffrey Skilling on the news of his resignation

✈ **BOTTOM LINE** ✈
He knew what he was doing.

JOSEPH BERARDINO

CEO, Arthur Andersen

CP Photo Archive: Stephen Boitano

The firm that figures out how to bring the knowledge and insights of two disciplines together to get the power of three, will be the real leader in this model. And we intend to be that leader.

—Business Times, *Singapore, February 20, 2001*

AFTERMATH: Andersen takes the lead in 1 + 1 = 3 accounting. When Andersen Enron partner David Duncan discovers the number 2, he shreds thousands of documents, hoping that others will remain unaware of the digit. But you can't keep 2 down. It surfaces in news reports and is asked to appear in front of Congress. Long-suffering 2 can no longer be silenced.

STRATEGY TO COMBAT DOWNTURN: As hiring Arthur Andersen as your auditor becomes like hiring R. Kelly as your baby-sitter, Berardino steps down. By the summer of 2002, Arthur Andersen stops auditing public companies.

BULL! The Big Five just turned into the Fat Four.

Bottom line? Apparently that depends on who your auditor is.

GERALD LEVIN

CEO, AOL Time Warner

CP Photo Archive: Nick Ut

AFTERMATH: AOL stock plunges from $50 to $9 in twenty-two months, and its $54 billion loss in the first quarter of 2001 is, at the time, the largest in the history of America.

STRATEGY TO COMBAT DOWNTURN: Resignation: "I want to put the poetry back in my life." The recent reduction of his bonus from $10 million to zero was a complete coincidence.

FUTURE PLANS: Applying his experience of collapsing AOL Time Warner to his new pursuit of poetry, he intends to merge two sonnets and end up with a haiku.

BULL! Made headlines by showing up at the announcement of the biggest merger in corporate history without a tie. After averaging $45 million a year in compensation, maybe he just couldn't afford one.

I have to say, and this is not an arrogant statement, the concept of putting these two companies together is profound.

—Business Week, *November 6, 2000*

⇥ **BOTTOM LINE** ⇤
You've got gall!

93

GARTH TURNER

Investment Guru, Canada

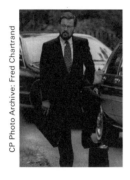

CP Photo Archive: Fred Chartrand

If you own Nortel, or a mutual fund holding it, don't bail out now. We are near, but not at, the low point. If you do not own Nortel, then this is the time to start accumulating it.

—Turner Report, *November 27, 2000*

AFTERMATH: Nortel goes from $32 a share to under a dollar.

RATIONALE: In that November 2000 report, Turner crows: "Nortel is massively profitable." Nortel had not reported a bottom-line profit in three years.

BULL! In a 2002 column about individual investors who lost on Nortel, Turner writes, "I am constantly amazed at the assumption people make that they can manage their own finances . . . most people can't. They don't have a clue how to pick stocks." When we set out to do this book, our lawyers advised us not to use the term [deleted by counsel]. Lord, give us strength.

⇥ **BOTTOM LINE** ⇤
[Deleted by counsel].

TOM HICKS

Owner, Texas Rangers

AL West Combined Standings 2001-2002

	W	L	Pct	GB
Seattle	209	115	.645	--
Oakland	205	119	.632	4
Anaheim	174	150	.537	35
Texas	145	179	.447	64

I do this for a living. I buy companies and build them and make them better.

—Following the record $252 million signing of Alex Rodriguez, December 2000

AFTERMATH: The Rangers rack up two last place seasons and $70 million in losses, amid accusations that Hicks's reckless spending epitomizes the destruction of baseball. The collapse of Hicks's telecom holdings leads to rampant speculation that he's running low on cash.

CAPITULATION: Though he once called owners who overspend on players "stupid," he goes on to run the Rangers' 2002 payroll to $105 million with massive salaries for lackluster talent. However, as the team fails, attendance flags, and losses follow, Hicks announces, "I'm not doing it anymore. We're going to play within our means from now on."

BULL! For twenty years, each eye-popping record baseball salary was quickly topped by another. But two years after Hicks went so far beyond any other bidder to nab ARod, there's nothing bigger on the horizon. If anything, big money signings are vanishing, as sane economics becomes the new priority.

BONUS QUOTE: "I've never shot a mammal." Is there no end to this guy's bragging?

⇒ **BOTTOM LINE** ⇒

Bought at the peak of the baseball bubble *and* the telecom bubble. Double play!

BRUNO COHEN

Senior Vice President, Business News, CNBC

CNBC Sept. to May 1997-2002

427 000
353 000
302 000
298 000
282 000

1997-98 1998-99 1999-00 2000-01 2001-02

No. of TV homes tuned to CNBC

You can't make a television appearance and then read four minutes of boilerplate. . . . We would probably resist anything the government would tell us to do with our programming.

—USA Today,
December 8, 2000

AFTERMATH: In 2001, the SEC demands that employees of financial companies disclose conflicts when talking stocks on TV.

BULL! Answering critics that CNBC participated in the bubble: "We're under no obligation to be boring. We think the financial markets and the economy are fascinating topics and make no apology for providing quality journalism."

THE RATINGS: Cohen was right the first time. Boilerplates make lousy television. But even boilerplates are better than bear markets. As stocks drop, *Broadcasting & Cable* reports CNBC's slip from the highest-rated cable channel to "trailing Fox News, CNN and MSNBC, and nearly even with Headline News."

STRATEGY TO COMBAT DOWNTURN: In August 2002, CNBC abandons its fancy digs at Carnegie Tower (the $125 per foot building Clinton couldn't afford) and moves to smaller, cheaper studios. Cohen announces that he's taking a four-month sabbatical and will not be returning. Some call that being fired. Others say it was the result of political infighting. Either way, no one is watching.

⊱═ **BOTTOM LINE** ═⊰
CNBC, Country's Nonstop Boilerplate Channel.

LIZ ANN SONDERS

Managing Director, Campbell, Cowperthwait

Wall Street's a funny place. It's the only sort of store that puts its things on sale, and everybody runs.

—*CNNfn*, Talking Stocks, *December 14, 2000*

AFTERMATH: On the same broadcast in which she implies that the public is stupid and she is smart, Sonders makes the following recommendations. JDS Uniphase (down 96 percent in the subsequent two years): "Love it both long term and short term"; AOL (68 percent): "This is going to be the premier dominant franchise media company"; Ciena (94 percent): "Going to be a winner"; Cisco (70 percent): "This is not an expensive stock"; Oracle (70 percent): "I think it should probably be a core holding in a portfolio"; Sun Microsystems (85 percent): "I think it absolutely should be a core holding"; Citigroup (40 percent): "We like Citi"; AIG (40 percent): "We like AIG"; and Morgan Stanley (50 percent): "Core holding." We're not leaving out the winners, that's the complete list.

BULL! Despite the vastly reduced prices, none of those great stocks are on her buy list when Louis Rukeyser asks for Sonders's technology picks in May 2002. She too runs from the sale, instead recommending Intel (down 50 percent in the next four months) and EDS (down 80 percent).

⊱ **BOTTOM LINE** ⊰

Wall Street in 2000: Sale! Wall Street in 2002: Everyday Low Prices!

LIZ ANN SONDERS
Managing Director, Campbell, Cowperthwait

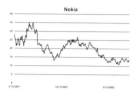

> I think if you have the appropriate long-term time horizon, three- to five-year time horizon, you're gonna look back at this and say, "What an amazing buying opportunity."
>
> —*CNBC*, Business Center, *February 15, 2001*

AFTERMATH: Stock prices correct dramatically over the next two years such that no long-term investor will ever look upon early 2001 as any kind of buying opportunity.

BULL! Just to show the previous Sonders page was no fluke, here are her stock picks from that February 15, 2001, edition of *Business Center*: Brocade Communications (down 75 percent within two years), BEA Systems (85 percent), Nokia (50 percent), Applied Biosystems (75 percent), and Enron (100 percent).

CAUTION: In 1999, Sonders warned against heeding the TV stock pickers: "Be careful in making investment decisions off a twenty-second comment from a portfolio manager who doesn't know anything about your own personal situation." Whose personal situation would've benefited from Sonders's picks? A Method actor preparing for a role in *Rent*?

RHONDA SCHAFFLER

Reporter, Anchor, CNNfn

Source: Nielsen Media Research

Okay. Great point, Liz Ann, thanks so much.

—*CNNfn*, Market Call, *March 1, 2001*

AFTERMATH: Liz Ann's great point proves to be, as usual, way off the mark.

HITS KEEP COMING: Schaffler tells Sonders: "You've pointed out a couple of times that if you've got a long-term horizon, there are some technology stocks you should own." She adds: "And people need to hear that." Well, it is true that in tough times people need a good laugh.

BULL! When Sonders dismisses rumors of an earnings disappointment at Veritas, Schaffler intones that, even if they do disappoint, "you're still looking at growth rates that exceed so many other companies'—even if it's 40 percent . . . as opposed to 50 percent—which people continue to lose sight of, when we watch what's going on in technology." Veritas had lost money in 2000 and loses even more in 2001 as the stock falls 80 percent from the time of Schaffler's sermon.

⇥ BOTTOM LINE ⇤
Viewers looking for objective financial journalism get Schaffted.

JEFFREY APPLEGATE

Chief Investment Strategist, Lehman Brothers

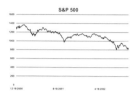

We started out the year being bullish. . . . But we would argue that the bulk of the correction is behind us, so now is the time to be offensive, not defensive.

—Florida Times-Union,
December 17, 2000

AFTERMATH: Applegate admits the dismal results of his predictions for 2000: "Being bullish. . . . That obviously looked wonderful until March 10. Through November 30, that looked pretty stupid. And we've also had a portfolio that is overweight tech, so we have obviously taken our lumps there." But like any good cult leader, he can't keep himself from chanting the mantra: Buy!

BULL! Applegate goes on to predict the S&P will hit 1,800 by the end of 2001. It closes down 200 points at 1,161. Applegate predicts it will end 2002 at 1,075, but as the year winds on, he revises his estimate to 1,200. By September 2002 it's at 889. By November 2002, Applegate is out of a job.

ROD SMYTH
Chief Investment Strategist, Wachovia Securities

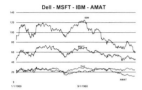

Dell - MSFT - IBM - AMAT

There is a risk they [his large-cap tech picks: Dell, Microsoft, Intel, IBM, and Applied Materials] could go lower, but if you buy at these prices and are patient, you will do fine.

—Chicago Tribune,
December 31, 2000

AFTERMATH: All of these stocks do spike at various times, but the trend for the long-term investor is bleak. After close to two years, only Dell is up, Intel is 50 percent down, and Applied Materials is 30 percent lower.

BULL! A few months later, Smyth says: "We reiterate our view that 'New Tech' stocks should not be sold at current levels. Investors will probably regret selling just as their valuations are becoming cheap and their stocks deeply oversold." Technically he's right, since the techs rally briefly, but his fundamentals look sketchy because he recommends selling large-cap techs in 2002, when they're considerably lower priced. How can Intel be fundamentally cheap at 25 and a sell at 17?

⊰⇒ **BOTTOM LINE** ⇒⊱

If you give your money to this Irishman, it won't be Dublin anytime soon!
(Three percent of the world's population really likes puns.
Let's throw them a bone here.)

ALAN GREENSPAN

Chairman, Federal Reserve Board/Knight

1999 Analyst Recommendations

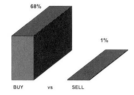

The three- to five-year average earnings projections of more than a thousand analysts, though exhibiting some signs of flattening in recent months, have generally held firm. Such expectations, should they persist, bode well for continued capital deepening and sustained growth."

—*Speech, New York, New York, December 2000*

AFTERMATH: The fantasy of tech earnings vaporizes, as does capital spending, as does economic growth. And, little by little, Greenspan's reputation evaporates too.

THE BIG QUESTIONS: Didn't we all think the great Alan Greenspan was using more than the same CEO and analyst tripe that everyone else was? What other sources was he using, AOL chat rooms? Is that briefcase just for show?

BULL! The corporate managers whose optimism Greenspan was celebrating were probably selling their own stock at that very moment. The analysts whose forecasts he hyped were shills for those corporate managers in exchange for lucrative investment banking business. All of this was well known on Wall Street, but apparently beyond the grasp of the most exalted economic figure of our lifetime. Or else Greenspan was just getting his own payoff in the form of widespread love and acceptance. Let's face it, Alan Greenspan probably didn't get to eat with the popular kids in high school.

⊱ **BOTTOM LINE** ⊰

Greenspan was seeing the wrong kind of analyst.

MICHAEL "WAXIE" PARNESS

Guru and Infomercial Star, Trendfund.com

2001 NFL Salaries Compared to Theismann

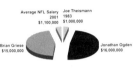

Ka-chingo!

—Long-running infomercial for Trend Trading

AFTERMATH: Thousands of insomniacs are convinced that the stock market is a sure-fire alternative to working for a living.

SAY IT AIN'T SO: Former Redskins QB Joe Theismann does the hosting honors, asking the probing question "Now, don't you need a lot of money to get started in *Trend Trading*?" (Answer below.) Luckily, sports salaries have escalated wildly since Theismann played, so today's NFL stars won't be reduced to this.

BULL! The program mentions Waxie's "number-one technical analyst 'Tiny,'" followed by a testimonial from a woman who says, "I really do believe in Waxie and Tiny." Wouldn't you rather be poor than ever utter that sentence?

FUN FACT: Even though he paid to star in one hour of programming that would run thousands of times, Waxie elected not to shave that day.

⇥═ **BOTTOM LINE** ═⇤

No, you don't need a lot of money to get started in *Trend Trading*!

SUZE ORMAN

Best-selling Author/Public Speaker/Host, CNBC, The Suze Orman Show

Nasdaq Composite

If you are in the NASDAQ—if you are in technology stocks, I would not be selling here. Now it is almost too late."

—*CNN*, Larry King Live, *January 2, 2001*

AFTERMATH: The NASDAQ, at 2,291 when Orman dispensed her wisdom to Larry King's now impoverished audience, would be hacked in half over the next twenty months.

STRATEGY TO COMBAT DOWNTURN: Orman insists that "you're in for the long haul." She forgets that Larry King's average viewer is eighty-three and the long haul is three weeks.

BULL! The first of Orman's many best-selling books is entitled *You've Earned It, Don't Lose It*. Of particular relevance is the fourth chapter, entitled "Disregard Me at All Times."

SUZE ORMAN

Best-selling Author/Public Speaker/Host, CNBC, The Suze Orman Show

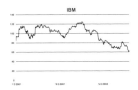

Safe, today, to me, truthfully, are still the good quality stocks: your Dow Jones stocks, your blue-chip stocks, your stocks like IBM.

—CNN, Larry King Live, *January 2, 2001*

AFTERMATH: The Dow Jones average loses roughly 30 percent of its value in the next eighteen months. IBM goes from over $90 a share to $65.

BULL! Orman has also written *The Courage to Be Rich*, *The Road to Wealth*, and *The 9 Steps to Financial Freedom*. Buyers of all three prove better off than those who buy only one, since their book bonfires provide more vitally needed heat after investing losses leave them unable to pay the gas company.

MORE BULL? Listen to *The Suze Orman Show* on radio stations across the country, including KQMO-FM in Shell Knob, Missouri, from 4:00 to 6:00 P.M. EST.

⇥ **BOTTOM LINE** ⇤

Safe, truthfully, is changing the channel when Suze is on. Which isn't easy, because she's always on.

SUZE ORMAN

Best-selling Author/Public Speaker/Host, CNBC, *The Suze Orman Show*

Dow Jones Industrial Average 1966-86

The markets will come back again; they always have. If you have five or ten years, you will be okay.

—*CNN,* Larry King Live, *January 2, 2001*

AFTERMATH: So far not good. And time does not heal all wounds.

BULL! If you bought the Dow Index in January 1966:

After five years, you were down 11 percent.
After ten years, you were down 35 percent.
After fifteen years, you were down 8 percent.
After twenty years, you were up 33 percent.

That 33 percent gain over twenty years is roughly 1.5 percent a year compounded. Over the same period, U.S. government Treasury Bills averaged 7 percent. It is possible for stocks to be the wrong choice over the much ballyhooed "long haul." And we didn't even have to cite the Great Depression.

MORE BULL! Suze is a contributing editor to Oprah Winfrey's *O* magazine. It was actually *2 Million Magazine* before Orman joined up, but she reduced it to *O*.

Larry King gets it right: "This woman is never wrong!"

SUZE ORMAN

Best-selling Author/Public Speaker/Host, CNBC, The Suze Orman Show

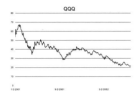

AOL, I think, is a fabulous company to be buying. I would have no problem buying it here.

—*CNN*, Larry King Live, *January 2, 2001*

AFTERMATH: AOL falls 72 percent in less than two years.

BULL! In 2002, the New Suze goes on a tear about an analyst who had been recommending AOL "since the late 1990s . . . '98, '99, it's a buy, buy it, the year 2000, buy it, the year 2001, buy it. . . . It has gone down 72 percent since he came out and he said buy." She ends the rant by saying, "This is an example of why you think you're going to financial advisers, you think you're going to people who really know more than you. But you've got to ask yourself the question: Do they really? Are you sure? Do you know without a shadow of a doubt that the information you're getting from these financial advisers is based in fact, is based in goodness, for you to make money out of? That you are going to make more by paying them a fee than simply doing it on your own? I have to tell you: I doubt it highly. And that is why *The Suze Orman Show* is here. . . . You can do anything that you want if you simply take a little bit of time and just keep listening, and just keep learning."

⊱ **BOTTOM LINE** ⊰
Unbelievable.

LARRY KING

Host, CNN, Larry King Live

CP Photo Archive: Reed Saxon

AFTERMATH: Only those viewers confused by King's double negative are spared a financial beating.

BULL! See pages 104 to 107.

**[On Suze Orman]
You can't afford
not to listen to
this woman.**

—*CNN*, Larry King Live,
January 2, 2001

You can't not be not broke if you haven't
not listened to advice not given by Larry King.

SUZE ORMAN
Best-selling Author/Public Speaker/Host, CNBC, The Suze Orman Show

In the low 60s here, I think [QQQ] they're a buy. They may go down, but if you dollar-cost average, where you put money every single month into them, I think, in the long run, it's the way to play the NASDAQ.

—*CNBC*, Business Center, *January 4, 2001*

AFTERMATH: The QQQ falls by another 64 percent. Averaging down into technology proves to be pouring money down a black hole.

REALITY CHECK: If you averaged down into the Qs every month, as Suze commanded, you'd need a bounce of 63 percent off the July 2002 low just to break even. And it could have much further to slide.

BULL! That same evening, in response to an e-mailer who asks if he should sell his stocks like his friends did, she says: "Get yourself a bunch of new friends. Losers!" Haven't heard that kind of talk since they took the get-rich-quick guy Tom Vu off the air.

━ **BOTTOM LINE** ━

Don't blame Suze. How could she have known that putting money every month into an index with massive valuations, low earnings, no dividends, and downward momentum would go so wrong? She's not a psychic, folks.

GEORGE W. BUSH
President/MBA

Nasdaq Composite

I do think people who have invested in this industry are, in the long term, going to realize good gains on the money they've invested, because this is the leading edge of thought in the world.

—*San Francisco tech conference, January 4, 2001*

AFTERMATH: The NASDAQ loses over 50 percent in the next two years as investors discover that there's a big difference between creating technology and creating profits.

FUZZY MATH: Chances of good gains for those who buy tech shares at the time of Bush's statement (or, worse, in the previous two years) have faded. Even if the NASDAQ gains 20 percent a year for five straight years beginning in 2003, it would still be only a 3 percent annual gain for the January 2001 buyers. And such growth on the NASDAQ is not a likely prospect when earnings and dividends are all the rage.

BULL! In March 2000, Bush says, "I'm sorry people are losing value in their portfolios, but with the right policies, I am confident our economy will recover" and "The American economy is like a great athlete at the end of the first leg of a long race: somewhat winded, but fundamentally strong." But by July 2002, Bush himself sounds winded: "You're talking to the wrong guy about what stocks to buy."

━━ **BOTTOM LINE** ━━
Even when it's leading edge, it's not the thought that counts.

STEVE FOLKER

Director of Equity Strategy, Fifth Third Bank

Broadwing

> **They [Broadwing] have a strong capability to develop new telecom services in strong growth areas . . . and their cash flow is still pretty strong.**
>
> —Business Courier,
> *January 5, 2001*

AFTERMATH: Despite the strong cash flow in 2000–2001 (free cash flow: negative $50 million), shares in Broadwing go from $28 at the time of Folker's endorsement to single digits a year later.

STRATEGY TO COMBAT DOWNTURN: While the largest institutional holder of Broadwing has bailed, in March 2002, Folker is hanging on to 2.6 million shares at $8 saying, "We're a little more willing to look farther out." A few months farther out, the stock is below $2.

BULL! In December 2000, Folker declares the stock market "undervalued" and urges investors to wade in. Strike one. In June 2001, he says it's time to "buy on weakness." Strike two. After a year of tumbling prices, Folker says rough economic times ahead are "mostly priced into the stocks already." Folker goes down swinging! But wait, he's still at the plate!

⇥ **BOTTOM LINE** ⇤

When it's other people's money, it's not a real ball game,
it's just batting practice.

JOHN ROTH

President and CEO, Nortel

CP Photo Archive: Tibor Kolley

Demand to our end carrier customers is not going away. . . . Our business is really well centered in areas of high growth.

—Dallas Morning News, *January 19, 2001*

AFTERMATH: Nortel lays off over 20,000 people in 2001 after they report a $19 billion loss. But their losses are no accounting scandal. They'd been reporting multibillion-dollar losses for years. For some reason, nobody, including analysts, much cared. Over the next year, the stock tumbles from $70 to a low of $0.97. In a review of top CEOs, the *National Post* muses about Roth: "Over the past twelve months, he's guided Nortel to the biggest loss in Canadian history yet in 2000 saw his compensation rise more than tenfold to $150 million."

STRATEGY: Like any seasoned partygoer, Roth leaves while things are swinging and announces his resignation six months before layoffs. "I will not be leaving until our annual meeting next year. . . . This gives us plenty of time to recruit a successor." The company says it will take a year to replace someone as experienced as Roth, but after a look at the books, they find a new CEO in four months.

BULL! Roth is quoted as saying, "A lot of people play defense. I prefer to play offense." Wayne Gretzky he ain't.

⇢ **BOTTOM LINE** ⇠
Offensive.

VINCE FARRELL

Chairman, Victory Capital

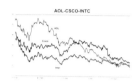

But say Intel has to test its bottom at $30 and Microsoft at $45 and AOL at $45 and Cisco Systems at $35. And I believe those bottoms are going to hold.

—*CNNfn*, Ahead of the Curve, *January 23, 2001*

AFTERMATH: AOL, Intel, and Cisco test their bottoms and land closer to $10.

BULL! To Farrell's credit, he follows his prediction with a warning, of sorts: "Now, to me, they're still too high, but I'm a value guy so I'm always going to think they're too high. . . . But I believe we're setting ourselves up for the opportunity to buy world-class companies at very good prices."

STRATEGY TO COMBAT DOWNTURN: As the stock market continues to fall, gurus offer fewer declarative statements. When asked if he stands by his July 2002 prediction, "I think we have hit a bottom," Farrell responds with self-deprecation: "For at least two minutes."

⇥ **BOTTOM LINE** ⇤
If you're going to give away two-thirds of your cash, give it to world-class companies.

JOHN RIGAS

Founder, Adelphia Communications

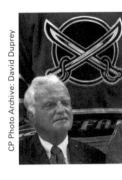

CP Photo Archive: David Duprey

Adelphia has positioned itself very well for the future. . . . We're here for the long pull because we think there is a lot of value and it's a great business.

—Buffalo News, *February 15, 2001*

AFTERMATH: The SEC charges Rigas, two sons, and two execs with inflating earnings while excluding billions in liability. The next day federal prosecutors charge that the Rigas clan "looted Adelphia on a massive scale using the company as the Rigas family's personal piggy bank." In September 2002 they charge them with twenty-four counts of wire fraud, bank fraud, securities fraud, and conspiracy in "one of the most elaborate and extensive corporate frauds in U.S. history," which in a year of elaborate and extensive corporate fraud is quite an achievement. Adelphia files for Chapter 11 while John Rigas does the perp walk.

BULL! Rigas's lawyer defends him by pointing out that "he has never sold a share of stock and . . . has never profited from Adelphia stock." Well, no. He didn't profit from the stock, but there is the small matter of the reported $13 million dollar golf course on Rigas property, the Mexican, Rocky Mountain, and New York homes, the three private jets, and African safaris. All paid for by cable viewers, who by reports pay high prices and who allegedly get lousy reception.

+= **BOTTOM LINE** =+
Service discontinued.

MARY FARRELL
Senior Investment Strategist, UBS PaineWebber

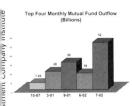

Top Four Monthly Mutual Fund Outflow
(Billions)

Source: Investment Company Institute

It looks like investors really are just across the board wanting to be invested in this market, and we're glad. We need a higher savings and investment rate in the U.S.

—*CNNfn*, Street Sweep,
December 16, 1999

AFTERMATH: Trillions of dollars in paper wealth evaporate almost overnight. Turns out there's a difference between savings, investment, and pyramid schemes.

STRATEGY: A presidential-style campaign. In early 2001 the *St. Petersburg Times* reports on Farrell's stump speech "to about 350 PaineWebber clients in Tampa as part of a weeklong swing through Florida." Her message: "We've got some rough sledding ahead with the economy slowing, but we believe this bull market continues." There are refreshments served, so it's not a total loss.

BULL! During one televised campaign stop, she suggests investors "step up to the plate" with the following "long-term holdings": Citigroup, AMEX, Johnson & Johnson, Verizon, JDS Uniphase, and Cisco. Five of the six will fall by over 50 percent during the next two years.

↠ BOTTOM LINE ↞

It's time for PaineWebber clients to ask: Are you better off now than you were four years ago?

115

MARY FARRELL

Senior Investment Strategist, UBS PaineWebber

CP Photo Archive: Denis Doyle

I think that points up a problem that I think your viewers should be aware of, and that's when they hear a recommendation on a program, they can't assume that that's a permanent recommendation.

—*CNNfn*, Business Center, *February 15, 2001*

AFTERMATH: Three of Farrell's four stock picks on that same broadcast close sharply lower the following day and never recover. But *do not blame Farrell*, you stupid viewers. These are not permanent recommendations. They are not meant to last through the entire *night*.

BULL! After being consistently wrong in her market projections for the first 30 months of this millennium, Farrell again chides the general public: "I think the market is ignoring the fundamentals. The fundamentals are actually very good."

BONUS QUOTE: In June 2002 she says, "You mentioned the sell recommendations on Wall Street. Many of them are way too late, especially in technology." In a month the NASDAQ is 20 percent lower. But hanging on to some tech stocks was not a permanent recommendation, simpletons!

We can't assume Farrell's recommendations are permanent.
But we can usually assume they're lousy.

MARIA BARTIROMO

Anchor, Reporter, CNBC

Yahoo!

I am of the belief that the individual out there is actually not throwing money at things that they do not understand, and is actually using the news and using the information out there to make smart investment decisions.

—*CNN*, Larry King Live, *March 2001*

AFTERMATH: Since most readers are still laughing, this paragraph will not contain commentary.

THROWING MONEY: At the end of 1999, Yahoo! has a market capitalization over twice the size of General Motors' despite having virtually no historical earnings.

BULL! Bartiromo is committed to the calling of financial journalism. In 2000 she tells *People*: "It would take a phenomenal position for me to consider leaving . . . and that's how I feel about the Kathie Lee spot."

BONUS FACT: Bartiromo is commonly referred to as the money honey, even though there are at least four better-looking women at CNBC. Five if you include Carl Quintanilla.

⇥ **BOTTOM LINE** ⇤
How do you solve a problem like Maria?

MARK DAMPIER

Head of Research, Hargreaves Lansdown

The FTSE 100 could test 5,000 in the short term, but these falls should be seen as long-term buying opportunities.

—*BBC Vision Radio, April 13, 2001*

AFTERMATH: The FTSE, Great Britain's benchmark stock index, goes from 5,760 to 3,609 in the next seventeen months. That's a level not seen since 1997.

BULL! Dampier's routine seems well rehearsed. As the NASDAQ began to sputter in April 2000, he advised, "For those investors prepared to take a long-term view, this market correction could be seen as a useful buying opportunity." Showing the caution so prevalent at the time, he added, "It's likely to be a pretty bumpy ride for the next few days, if not weeks."

CONGRATULATIONS: The Hargreaves web site proudly states that Dampier has been named 2001's "Most Frequently Quoted Pundit." There's one that eluded Archbishop Desmond Tutu. "The one that got away," he called it bitterly.

✦ **BOTTOM LINE** ✦

It's not easy to sound stupid with a London accent. Well done, mate.

ABBY JOSEPH COHEN

Chief Investment Strategist, Goldman Sachs

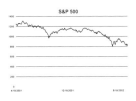

The time to be nervous was a year ago. The S&P then was overvalued; it's now undervalued. Then, profits were just beginning to decelerate; now, we think they're beginning to stabilize and reaccelerate.

—*CNN*, Lou Dobbs
Moneyline, *April 18, 2001*

AFTERMATH: Nerves remain frayed through 2001, and alcohol sales rise in 2002. Meanwhile the S&P, undervalued or not, loses 350 points over the next eighteen months.

STRATEGY TO COMBAT DOWNTURN: Through 2002, AJC reminds interviewers, "In March 2000 I advised your listeners to sell stocks" and "In March 2000, the day the S&P 500 hit its peak, we suggested to our clients that they sell some stocks." And "I can assure you that it is nothing compared to the criticism that we received in March of 2000 when we suggested to clients they take some money out of the stock market." That March 2000 suggestion: a reduction in her clients' stock holdings from 70 percent of their portfolios to 65 percent, a reduction of 5 percent. We repeat: 5 percent.

BULL! In late 2001, AJC's S&P forecast is 1,300. Twelve months later the S&P hangs around 800. Last we heard she was still calling for a twelve-month of 1,150. From 835, that's a pretty heady reacceleration.

✠ **BOTTOM LINE** ✠
Does "vroom, vroom"qualify as strategy?

JOSEPH NACCHIO

CEO and Chairman, Qwest Communications

CP Photo Archive: Ed Andrieski

Our competitors are blaming everything on the economy for not making their numbers. . . . It may be harder, but we're doing what we get paid to do.

—*On reporting 2001 first-quarter earnings,* Denver Business Journal, *April 24, 2001*

AFTERMATH: What exactly was Qwest paying Nacchio to do? Lay off over 7,000 employees, field an investigation by the SEC, and watch Qwest's credit rating downgrade to junk while the stock free-falls 90 percent. Apparently so, because at the end of 2001, Nacchio takes a $1.5 million bonus. In 2002 he cries foul, blaming "Enronitis" and "corporate McCarthyism." His reasoning? "If these things weren't in the press, they wouldn't have asked." Notably, Nacchio was not complaining about the press while Qwest's stock climbed.

BULL! Since 1999 Nacchio has sold over $266 million in Qwest stock.

REASON FOR RESIGNATION: "After criss-crossing the globe for five and one-half grueling years to build Qwest, living in two different cities, and having achieved our major goals, I have expressed my desire to spend more time with my family and pursue other opportunities."

✦══ **BOTTOM LINE** ══✦

Spending more time with the family? The kids better hide the piggy bank.

ARTHUR LAFFER

Supply-Side Economist

If anything, stock prices are now a little below fair value.

—American Spectator,
May 1, 2001

AFTERMATH: The S&P 500, Laffer's index of choice for measuring equity values, falls another 36 percent in the next year. More than half of the decline occurs before September 11, even though that tragedy becomes a popular excuse for bulls everywhere.

BULL! If the S&P was undervalued in May 2001, what does Laffer call it in 2002 when it's 36 percent lower? "Way undervalued, I'd guess by 40 or 50 percent. . . . I think we're going to have a very nice rally in the market over the next year or year and a half." Laffer made the comment to his fawning protégé Larry Kudlow on CNBC. If the interview hadn't been via satellite, there easily could've been lovemaking.

CLAIM TO FAME: Laffer is a former Reagan adviser who is best known for inventing the Laffer Curve, a graph depicting how higher taxes can reduce government revenue. He also runs Laffer Associates, an economic consulting firm. He is not connected with Laffer's, a comedy club in Denver.

≈ **BOTTOM LINE** ≈
Laffer is not the best medicine.

NED RILEY

Chief Investment Strategist, State Street Global Advisors

The name of the game is still earnings and it's still growth. I think the money will have to come back to that momentum, growth earnings, which is the large-cap tech stocks. I am always a contrarian, in that perspective.

—*CNN*, Moneyline, *May 4, 2001*

AFTERMATH: The money does not come back to the large-cap techs, because the public realizes what Ned did not: those companies had little earnings and no growth.

STRATEGY TO COMBAT DOWNTURN: Give Ned Riley credit, he's going down with the ship. He has stuck with his recommendation of the QQQ (large-cap tech stock composite shares) every step of the way down, standing by the once-popular notion that technology always leads the recovery. No Lou Dobbs–style chameleon act for Ned.

BULL! In September 2002, Riley went so far as to tell a CNN audience that he'll be recommending the QQQ "until the day I die."

➤ **BOTTOM LINE** ➤
Ned Riley, QQQ, we now pronounce you man and wife.

PRINCE AL-WALEED BIN TALAL BIN ABDULAZIZ AL-SAUD

Saudi Prince

I wrote him [Warren Buffett] a letter, you know, showing that I was, quote, the Buffett of Arabia.

—*CNBC*, Business Center, *May 16, 2001*

AFTERMATH: Buffett shows his usual humility, writing back, "I'm the Al-Waleed of Omaha." (True story.) However, Buffett would never invest heavily in high-profile tech stocks like AOL, Amazon, and Priceline, nor would he share the prince's penchant for day trading.

BULL! After making $10 billion on a successful bet on Citicorp in the mid-'90s, Al-Waleed endures substantial paper losses on the Internet stocks, EuroDisney, and Planet Hollywood. His Citigroup stake also gets socked by the market correction, and his ardent buy-and-hold philosophy cannot save his investments in WorldCom and KirchMedia, both bankrupt.

BONUS QUOTE: To a CNBC reporter in 2001: "So, please, I ask you to stop hammering Priceline."

≈ **BOTTOM LINE** ≈

The Speculator Formerly Known as Prince.

JOHN LAYFIELD

"Bradshaw," Wrestler-Investor, WWE

I believe the spinning off of [WorldCom's] consumer long-distance business is a great thing for them. I believe right now, it's one of the best long-distance companies, data companies, and a P/E of around 13, and growth's expected about 16 to 18 percent. I think it's going to be a great buy.

—*CNBC*, Squawk Box,
June 26, 2001

AFTERMATH: WorldCom, along with a host of other Layfield favorites, including Applied Materials and Oracle, takes a beating. In this ring, the beating is real. No fakes here, folks.

BULL! "I told myself after my football career was over that if I ever started making good money again I would invest it wisely." Where Oracle and WorldCom fit into "wisely" isn't clear. The 2001 volatility doesn't intimidate Layfield, who likes to toss off that he's writing a book about financial advice: "I've got all the chapters laid out; now all I have to do is write it." *SmackDown!* seems as good a title as any other.

✠ **BOTTOM LINE** ✠
CNBC: It's not sports or news . . . it's financial entertainment.

124

LEE HOLLINGSWORTH

Analyst, Hollingsworth & Co. Investments

I consider myself—and sell my services—as a professional financial analyst, but you can't figure fraud and deception into the equation. It's implied, when you have a prominent board of directors, that [fraud] is taken out of the equation.

—Atlanta Business Chronicle, *July 27, 2001*

AFTERMATH: Mr. Hollingsworth—and his clients—learn that "prominent board" and aboveboard are not always the same thing.

STRATEGY TO COMBAT DOWNTURN: Sell your house. Try to save your business.

BULL! Hollingsworth invested in World Access, an Atlanta-based long-distance carrier, and he advised his clients to do the same. What's the problem? A lawsuit claims that World Access was involved in a fraudulent plan to erase a $165 million debt left off World-Com's books to enhance their balance sheet before the MCI merger. World Access gets promise of contract. WorldCom gets World Access shares. Everybody goes bankrupt.

✠ **BOTTOM LINE** ✠
P/E less F + D.

ALAN SKRAINKA

Chief Investment Strategist, Edward Jones & Co.

Dow Jones Industrials 1929-34

My father saw a world where people were waiting to see the next big market crash, while my generation was raised on the idea of long-term equity investing.

—Los Angeles Times,
January 1, 2000

AFTERMATH: The next big market crash.

BULL! After the Dow hit 10,000, Skrainka described it as a "golden age for investors" and said, "This is going to impact my generation just like the Depression and the stock market crash affected my father's generation." Why he assumed the '20s stock mania would have one ending and the '90s stock mania another is hard to fathom.

FEARLESS FORECAST: April 2002: "The recession is over. Alan Greenspan has said a recovery is well under way. . . . If you look at history, the market has always ended higher twelve months after the end of a recession, with no exceptions to that rule in the past fifty years." Now there's one exception.

BONUS QUOTE: March 2000: "Well, in technology, we like companies like Lucent that certainly are helping build the Internet . . . that's a good opportunity. MCI WorldCom is certainly benefiting from the growth on the Internet . . . that's a good opportunity. So we're not saying stay away from the New Economy stocks, we are just saying buy the established companies that have a track record of earnings and that are trading at a smart price."

✦ **BOTTOM LINE** ✦
Golden age for short sellers.

STANLEY NABI
Managing Director, Credit Suisse Asset Management

Tyco

Some people have learned to shout "fire" in the middle of a packed movie. At Enron maybe there was fire, but in the case of Tyco and similar companies there is no fire.

—TheStreet.com, January 20, 2002

AFTERMATH: Fire!

STRATEGY TO COMBAT DOWNTURN:
Nabi, who TheStreet.com reports started buying Tyco in the mid-$30s, continues to offer a healthy prognosis: "I cannot believe that if you raise the hood on this operation you're going to see cancer there. I think you're only going to see minor blemishes."

BULL! Sticking with the mixed metaphor, the market mechanics come up with a different diagnosis. Cancer! Tyco hits a low of $7. Nabi turns to therapy talk: "The market is facing too many problems. But many of these are not fundamental, but psychological and political." And, "The shorts are playing a game. It's destabilized the market at a time when we need to get our sanity back." Why do they complain about whispers and rumors only when the stock is going down?

≈ **BOTTOM LINE** ≈
The doctor is in but the car is still broken.

THOMAS BAILEY

CEO, Janus Capital Management

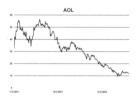

I'm the CEO. As long as it is fun for me, I don't see any reason why I have to leave. We have to get the numbers back. This is just about numbers.

—Investor's Business Daily, *December 11, 2001*

AFTERMATH: The numbers don't come back. Janus, which invested heavily in tech—Cisco, AOL Time Warner, Nokia, Enron—loses 50 percent of its assets in under two years. Which might be what happens to guys who say, "This is just about numbers." What else would it be about?

STRATEGY TO COMBAT DOWNTURN: After selling back his stake in the fund for $603 million, Bailey steps down.

BULL! We'll give this one to another fund manager, Jack Brennan: "From 1997 to 1999, having a diversified business didn't look all that attractive—if you were just in growth stocks, your assets were zooming. But if you look at what's happened over the past two years to the concentrated firm versus the diversified firm, the financial picture is clearly different."

⊹⊱ **BOTTOM LINE** ⊰⊹
It wasn't fun.

LARRY KUDLOW

Host, *CNBC*, Kudlow and Cramer/*Economist/Republican Adviser*

Photo: Associated Press: Tom Reed

The shock therapy of decisive war will elevate the stock market by a couple thousand points.

—National Review Online, *June 26, 2002*

AFTERMATH: Kudlow—who has no military record we're aware of—continues to vigorously demand an invasion of Iraq, with his favorite refrain being that we should attack Saddam Hussein "yesterday."

BULL! "Could it be that a lack of decisive follow-through in the global war on terrorism is the single biggest problem facing the stock market and the nation today? I believe it is." Kudlow's rationale for war draws a slight on-air rebuke from his CNBC colleague Consuelo Mack, who agrees with an invasion "but not for that reason."

DESPERATION: Kudlow's lives-for-points plan could stem from his floundering forecast that, by 2010, the NASDAQ will hit 10,000 and the Dow 35,000.

⇒ **BOTTOM LINE** ⇒
If Kudlow will be the first man into Baghdad, we're for it.

HILLARY CLINTON
Senator (D–NY)

CP Photo Archive: Gerald Lopez-Cepero

The 1990s, economically, was not a fluke or a bubble. If all the arrows pointing up are now pointing down, blame cannot be placed at the feet of those who led our nation during one of its greatest periods of prosperity and progress in its history.

—*Democratic Leadership Council meeting, July 29, 2002*

AFTERMATH: InvestorWords.com defines a bubble as "a description of rapidly rising equity prices, usually in a particular sector, that some investors feel is unfounded. The term is used because, like a bubble, the prices will reach a point at which they pop and collapse violently."

BLAME GAME: Clinton goes on to complain, "The Republican economic strategy has consisted of two things: bigger tax cuts and weaker regulations."

BULL! What about Bill's repeal of the Glass-Steagall Act, opening the door for financial industries to merge, acquire, and stick their $300 million lobbied fingers into all the money pies? The original act, created after the 1929 crash, was designed to discourage large companies from manipulating and corrupting a bull market. In essence, the act was meant to thwart "irrational exuberance." Great strategy. Open up the vault, leave the bank, and then blame the robbers.

⊱ **BOTTOM LINE** ⊰
It wasn't a bubble?

CHARLES E. SCHUMER

Senator (D–NY)

CP Photo Archive: Rick Bowmer

There has been no public debate on the issues limiting the activities of auditing accounting firms, and yet the SEC is not only proclaiming the need for such limits, but has proposed a rule which would curtail accounting firms' business models.

—*1999, as reported in* Accounting Today, *July 10, 2000*

AFTERMATH: Arthur Levitt's 1999 SEC attempt to curtail the accounting industry's practice of consulting for the same firms they are auditing turns into an "intensive and venal lobbying campaign" after the Big Five spend almost $14 million in contributions. Over forty senators write letters complaining about the proposal, calling it, among other things, "draconian." The House votes it down.

BULL! According to TheHill.com and Open Secrets, none other than Senator Charles E. Schumer heads the list of donation recipients, with $57,500. From 1989 to 2001, Schumer was the second largest recipient of accounting dough, with a grand total of $340,006.

THE SIGN OF A GOOD MIND: Not one to let two opposing ideas get in his way, Schumer takes up "religion" when accounting abuse hits the papers: "One of the best things we can do is have a tough SEC." More backpedaling: "It's our message to the House. It's our message to the president. If you really want to clean up the system, you have to do something with teeth."

+≥ **BOTTOM LINE** ≥+

Some things with teeth come back to bite you on the ass.

HENRY WEINGARTEN

Financial Astrologer and Founder, Astrologers Fund

Photo: The Astrologers Fund

International Hi-Tech Industries. It's a bulletin-board stock, and the stars say it's going to the moon.

—New York Post,
October 9, 2000

AFTERMATH: Before International Hi-Tech goes to the moon, it visits the basement . . . 27 cents, down from 76 cents.

BULL! Weingarten asserts that "the majority of money managers and traders in the world use financial astrology." Why do we believe him? He also claims that Saturn, "as you may know, represents the accounting industry." Okay. Then how do the stars sum it up? "Anybody who doesn't see that this market is driven by emotion . . . is just crazy. It is all about confidence."

Finally, a man who speaks the truth.

BEN STEIN

TV Personality and Economist

Photo: Comedy Network

$5000

Some bubble. You can't prick it with a steam shovel.

—Washington Post, *February 28, 1999*

AFTERMATH: Shovels aren't particularly effective on bubbles. Pinpricks are. Just over a year later, when there is a "slight uptick in inflation," the bubble breaks. By then Stein happily admits that whatever he made "was all taken away from me."

BULL! In Stein's single foray into the madness, he tracks his transformation from diligent P/E guy to bubble buyer. He can't help pointing out that he knows it's an illusion: "Maybe the prices are ridiculous and not real. In fact, I know they are." He closes with the warning "Likely, this will all end in tears." It is easy to discount analysts, but what do you do with doom-'n'-gloom guys like Stein? How does a reader square the writer of *A License to Steal: Michael Milken and the Conspiracy to Bilk the Nation* with "Federal law prohibits gambling on the Web—for now. But gambling with Web stocks works just as well." It's one thing when a stripper takes off her schoolgirl uniform, it's quite another when a schoolgirl does.

✄ **BOTTOM LINE** ✄

When Ben Stein is excited, you know something is wrong.

RON INSANA

Anchor, CNBC

DJIA 1963-1983

Now some people look at descriptions like the one you just offered and point to other times in the past, 1968 and, maybe even more worrisome, 1929, where the psychology was the same.

—*To Richard Grasso, CNBC, Business Center, March 29, 1999*

AFTERMATH: NYSE Chairman Dick Grasso replies that, though corrections will occur, investors have become "sophisticated," so things will be fine.

SKEPTIC: Insana, an avid market historian, has always been willing to rise above CNBC's reputed market boosterism. In 2001, when Suze Orman trots out a chart of the S&P's 400 percent return since 1987, Insana says: "Let me ask you about that, though, because some people believe that, even from 1981, the market's been in something of an anomalous period."

BULL! Faced with similar charts from Orman a month earlier, Insana's colleague Sue Herera says, "Okay. You ready to go to Piermont?" and takes the next caller's question.

BONUS FACT: This is presumably irrelevant, but Insana is one letter away from Insane.

↠ **BOTTOM LINE** ↞
They don't put a bald guy on network TV anymore unless he's really smart.

ALEX WINCH

President, Grange Research Corp.

Photo: Alex Winch

While this might seem to be a conservative accounting policy because it defers the booking of profits, it is in fact a very aggressive policy. . . . Drabinsky's life and company are interesting. But conservative they are not.

—Forbes,
September 25, 1995

AFTERMATH: When Winch responds to a glowing *Forbes* profile of Livent with a cautionary letter categorizing Livent cofounders Garth Drabinsky and Myron Gottlieb's former accounting practices at Cineplex Odeon as "aggressive," Drabinsky promptly sues Winch for $10 million.

STRATEGY TO COMBAT DOWNTURN: After paying $270,000 CDN in legal fees, Winch settles out of court. He steps down as president of Grange and shuts down the hedge fund. As agreed in the settlement, he apologizes in *Forbes*, the *Globe and Mail*, and the *Wall Street Journal*. If that weren't enough, for three years he's silenced on the subject of Livent. Canadian libel laws remain in place, as does Drabinsky. A chill settles over an already chilly country.

VINDICATION: In April 1998 Michael Ovitz and Roy Furman take over Livent and quickly discover what the SEC investigation later calls "an accounting fraud designed to inflate earnings, revenues, and assets." In August 1998 the Livent board dumps Drabinsky and Gottlieb. Three months later Livent declares bankruptcy. Winch was right.

⇒ **BOTTOM LINE** ⇐
Ruined but right.

MIKE MAYO

Banking Analyst, Credit Suisse First Boston Corp.

Photo: Prudential

Sell.

—1999

AFTERMATH: Mayo "was not terminated for issuing negative research. The decision to terminate Mayo was made solely by the management of CSFB's equity research department." The fact that he issued sells on banks that were CSFB clients was incidental.

BULL! Recent spate of investigations aside, analysts who issue sells are subject to threats of physical violence, loss of investment banking business, alienation at work, nasty phone calls, and of course, being fired. Mayo turns up at Prudential. One of the reasons he goes there is that they aren't known for their investment bankers. As nature abhors a vacuum—well, okay, maybe just magazine editors abhor a vacuum—Mayo is now profiled as the new star analyst and "anti-Blodget."

⊱ **BOTTOM LINE** ⊰
Sold but didn't sell out.

BARTON BIGGS

Chief Global Strategist, Morgan Stanley

I think Mr. Market is on drugs, maybe even heroin.

—Sydney Morning Herald, *November 8, 1999*

AFTERMATH: Mr. Market enters rehab. The Dow and NASDAQ begin their spectacular crashes just months after Biggs warns that large-cap U.S. stocks are "grossly overpriced and dangerous." His recession prediction also proves correct.

BULL! Biggs's sober precrash analysis leaves him as one of the few Wall Street big shots with any credibility. So the financial world snaps to attention when he turns bullish during the July 2002 market meltdown. He is a little early with his call, so his clients likely benefit little from the 1,000+ point rally that Biggs correctly expects, but the downside lashing they are spared from 2000 to 2002 presumably makes up for that. Biggs expresses optimism for a market recovery.

MOB RULE: In December 1999, Robert Reitzes of Bear Stearns sneers: "I don't dislike him. But I just would never have made any money following Barton Biggs." More of the genius of Robert Reitzes appears earlier in this book.

꘎═ **BOTTOM LINE** ═꘎

Mr. Market should have more friends who aren't enablers.
And who use the respectful title Mr.

JONATHAN JOSEPH

Analyst, Salomon Smith Barney

Photo: Salomon Smith Barney

Though a slowdown may take six to nine months, we see "first mover" evidence of a trend reversal in decelerating industry [semiconductor] unit shipments.

—National Post,
July 6, 2000

AFTERMATH: Joseph's downgrade from outperform to neutral bears out. Over the next nine months, the Philadelphia Semiconductor Index (SOXX) loses a third of its value. People start to e-mail Joseph death threats.

THE PERILS OF PAULINE: Sometimes you just have to feel sorry for the analysts. The investment side leans on them to pitch stocks they hate, brokers depend on them to be neutral, while TV encourages the idea that analysts work for consumers. No wonder they never issue sells.

➤ **BOTTOM LINE** ➤
Ladies, gentlemen . . . analysts are not wizards,
just geeks made good. Please, no more halos or death threats.

SANDRA BULLOCK

Actor

CP Photo Archive: Chris Pizello

[On Dow 10,000] No way? Oh, my God. I'm so glad you told me that. It's, like, I don't care.

—*CNBC*, Dow 10,000 Special, *March 29, 1999*

AFTERMATH: The reporter says, "You don't care at all?" And Bullock elaborates: "I don't care." Spoken like someone who still has her savings.

BULL! In the same broadcast, Yankees Manager Joe Torre opines, "Ten thousand, I think, was inevitable." He's the only person to spit on CNBC that day. But that was before Jim Cramer worked there.

BONUS FACT: Bullock didn't care when the Nikkei hit 10,000 either.

Don't blame Sandra Bullock for this stock market mess. *Speed 2* is a different story.

WILLIAM FLECKENSTEIN

President, Fleckenstein Capital/Columnist, RealMoney.com

Photo: Fleckenstein Capital Management

What's not going to be funny is what comes next. We've precipitated the greatest bubble in the history of the planet.

—Seattle Times, *December 12, 1999*

AFTERMATH: The bubble bursts in 2000, but in 2002 "Fleck" insists the worst of the fallout is yet to come.

FED UP: Fleck cites the "reckless" and "irresponsible" Alan Greenspan as the bubble's main culprit. After almost daily anti-Greenspan rants for years, in 2002 Fleck declares that Greenspan is "yesterday's news" and vows never to mention his name again in his column. He keeps the promise only by devising increasingly bizarre code names, such as "the two-legged recipient of multiple downgrades in this column." (Honest.)

MOB RULE: Fleck routinely uses "volume of hate mail" as a sell signal and is scolded by Lou Dobbs in 2001 for engaging in the "Un-American" pursuit of short selling.

Revenge of Fleckenstein. Now playing through 2010.

BOB KUTTNER

Coeditor, American Prospect

DJIA 1950-2002

Sometimes stocks have been depressed in this century for as long as twenty-five years. And people ought to keep that in mind.

—*CNN,* Crossfire,
December 21, 1999

AFTERMATH: Kuttner is looked upon as a lunatic spoilsport by the left and the right on *Crossfire* that night, and likely by the viewing audience. By 2002 his proposition is taken seriously by a very large minority.

YOU WERE WARNED: In March 2000, just ten days after the NASDAQ's peak, Kuttner writes: "The 1920s and 1930s, let's recall, were also an era of amazing technological breakthrough—in radio, television, telephone, electric power generation, mass production, and aviation—and none of it was sufficient to counteract catastrophe when investors lost confidence and financial markets unwound."

OPTIMIST! Kuttner diverges from many of the hard-core bears. In late 2000 he writes: "History will surely judge Greenspan as an exceptionally successful Fed chairman." By 2001 he still maintains hope that a severe downturn can be sidestepped with shrewd policy.

＊ **BOTTOM LINE** ＊
Worst case scenario: Three years down, twenty-two to go.
So buy the dips, people.

L. M. MAC DONALD

Coauthor, Bull!

Photo: Rev. Luke A. Murphy

Hey, Keith, I got in. This IPO thing is a cinch!

—February 8, 2000

AFTERMATH: Buy.com sinks from Mac Donald's intro price of $26.50 to zero. Bernie Ebbers makes $40,000.

STRATEGY TO COMBAT DOWNTURN: Watch friends get rich on ISCO and buy on the way down. Average in and buy more. Watch it sink to $0.25. Ask yourself, "What is a superconductor anyway?"

BULL! When Mac Donald tells her brother she's bought stock, he calls his broker and sells everything. So does his broker. Mac Donald begins watching CNBC on her computer, while checking the Datek streamer and trying to hold down a job. When her boss—who is already stupidly rich—notices, he calls his broker and sells everything. So does his broker. Many claim that Mac Donald's entry into the market precipitated an $8 trillion sell-off. Mac Donald remains sanguine: "The market is still searching for bottom. I can't wait until they get here."

⇒ **BOTTOM LINE** ⇒
If she's in, you're out.

GREG ECKLER

Coauthor, Bull!

Photo: D. Eckler

I like to own companies that start with letters far apart in the alphabet. That way, when the ticker is rolling by, one of my stocks is always coming up.

—*Over dinner, 1998*

AFTERMATH: Most televised stock tickers switch from an alphabetic listing to live, real-time trades, so the entire Eckler investing system is rendered useless. A book on the system is scrapped at the manuscript stage.

BULL! In 2000 Eckler discovers fuel cells, snapping up Ballard Power Systems at a bargain $60 against his father's stern warning that companies with no profits in their history are not worth $5 billion. Eckler Jr.'s brilliance becomes clear as the stock hits $100. Less clear when it hits $10. Eckler Sr. explains that "whether it's fuel cells or flying cars, until there's a profit, it's just a story." And "Through the ages, idiots have been sucked in by good stories." And "How dare you defy me, I've been investing for forty years. You're snarky and foolish. Sit back down, pinhead, I'm just getting started."

≈ **BOTTOM LINE** ≈

Ballard would be at $200 today if Eckler Sr. wasn't *rooting* for his son to fail.

ACKNOWLEDGMENTS

Even humble little books such as *Bull!* need a lot of help to find their way into the world. The authors would like to thank some of those people now. It's always so nice to see your name in print, don't you think? To Donna Eckler and Rev. Luke A. Murphy . . . many thanks. To Sue Mullins, Steve Fishman, Sled Dog, Susie Reiss, Allison Outhit, Robert Kapanen, and the Reverand for research, graph help, advice, and connections. To our agent, James Vines, who answered a lonely e-mail and envisioned *Bull!* from the get-go. Hell, he could have written it. To everyone at Andrews McMeel, who added a book to their list at the last moment without complaint. And to all the people who provided photos to us. But, especially, to Eckler Sr., without whom this book would not exist.

SOURCES

ACAMPORA: "The silence is troubling . . ." *Columbus Dispatch*, December 24, 2000; "I'm a trend follower . . ." *New York Daily News*, December 29, 2000; "When you have companies . . ." BBC World Service, March 20, 1999; "The year 2000 . . ." BBC News Online, December 30, 1999; "Peace is bullish . . ." *The Fourth Mega-Market*, 1999. Other Sources: *Agence France-Presse*, January 4, 2000; *New York Observer*, December 4, 2000; Nexis.com.

APPLEGATE: Other Sources: *Palm Beach Post*, November 9, 2001; *Financial Times*, July 27, 2002; CNN, *Moneyline Weekend*, July 6, 2002.

BAILEY: "From 1997 to 1999 . . ." *Fortune*, September 30, 2002. Other Sources: *New York Times*, September 22, 2002; *Investor's Business Daily*, December 11, 2001; TheStreet.com, June 12, 2002.

BARBASH: Other Source: *Washington Post*, June 22, 2001.

BARTIROMO: "It would take a phenomenal position . . ." *Fortune*, May 29, 2000.

BATTIPAGLIA: "I think technology . . ." CNNfn, *Street Sweep*, October 24, 2000; "I think we've seen . . ." CNNfn, *Street Sweep*, September 4, 2002.

BERARDINO: Other Source: *Kitchener-Waterloo Record*, September 3, 2002.

BIGGS: "grossly overpriced . . ." TheStreet.com, November 11, 1999; "I don't dislike him . . ." CNN, *Moneyweek*, December 18, 1999. Other Source: *Nightly Business Report*, July 11, 2002.

BLODGET: "Can we please reset . . ." *Australian Financial Review*, June 15, 2002; "dogs . . ." NBC, *Take the Money and Run*, July 28, 2002; "Regrets that there were instances . . ." ML.com, May 21, 2002; "I kind of felt . . ." *Seattle Post-Intelligencer*, November 16, 2001. Other Source: *Sunday Times* (London), April 14, 2002.

BURNHAM: "So far as I know . . ." CNNfn, *Money Gang*, April 12, 2001; "I think Siebel is an attractive stock . . ." CNNfn, *Money Gang*, June 12, 2001; "Companies . . . will come back . . . CNNfn, *Street Sweep*, December 6, 2001; "Siebel Systems is another company . . ." CNNfn, *Street Sweep*, January 21, 2002.

BUSH: "If they buy stock . . ." *Weekly Compilation of Presidential Documents*, July 29, 2002; "Ninety-five percent of people . . ." *Time*, July 22, 2002; "I'm sorry . . ." CNN, *Inside Politics*, March 14, 2001; "The American economy is like . . ." CNN, *Inside Politics*, March 27, 2001; "You're talking to the wrong guy . . ."

Hamilton Spectator, July 23, 2002. Other Sources: Agence France-Presse, January 23, 2002; *Houston Chronicle,* June 21, 2002.

CARLSON: "I've always wondered this . . ." and "corporate malfeasance" CNN, *Crossfire,* July 12, 2002; "Cisco Systems reported . . ." CNN, *Crossfire,* September 2, 2002.

CHADWICK: "I think it's essential . . ." CNNfn, *Ahead of the Curve,* December 2, 1999; "Well, I do think . . ." CNNfn, *Ahead of the Curve,* April 6, 2000; "This stock market has had . . ." CNNfn, *Ahead of the Curve,* December 13, 2000; "Definitely not a recession . . ." CNNfn, *Ahead of the Curve,* December 27, 2000; "I don't think so . . ." CNNfn, *Ahead of the Curve,* February 24, 2000.

CHENEY: "I've been out . . ." CBS Debate, October 5, 2000; "A horrible mistake . . ." *Washington Post,* August 11, 2002; "One of the most exciting things . . ." *Boston Globe,* June 2, 2002; "As we go into 2000 . . ." *Aberdeen Press and Journal,* May 22, 1999; "I get good advice . . ." www.bbc.co.uk, 1996; "is under SEC scrutiny . . ." *Wall Street Journal,* July 15, 2002; "There are editorial writers . . ." *Boston Globe,* August 8, 2002. Other Sources: TheStreet.com, August 9, 1999; *American Prospect,* August 22, 2002; *New York Times,* August 24, 2002.

CLINTON: "If Mr. Greenspan should happen to die . . ." CNN, *Crossfire,* December 21, 1999; "Hopefully he doesn't nick himself . . ." CNN, *Larry King Live,* January 2, 2001; "The Republican economic strategy . . ." www.clinton.senate.gov; "irrational exuberance" White House Bulletin, August 30, 2002. Other Sources: opensecrets.org; Federal Reserve Bulletin, August 8, 2000.

COHEN: "We're under no obligation. . ." *Chicago Tribune,* July 28, 2002; "Trailing Fox News . . ." *Broadcasting & Cable,* August 12, 2002. Other Sources: *USA Today,* December 8, 2000; *New York Post,* August 14, 2002.

CRAMER: "I think that we are entering . . ." Realmoney.com, July 24, 2002; "Yahoo!, AOL, SUNW . . ." Yahoo! Chat, February 10, 2000; "I like SUNW!" RealMoney.com, December 28, 2000; "The worst is indeed over . . ." Realmoney.com, January 19, 2001; "For too long . . ." RealMoney.com, August 28, 2001. Other Sources: *Dayton Daily News,* January 11, 2000; Siliconvalley.com, December 4, 2000; Newyork.com, March 31, 2001; TheStreet.com, February 4, 2000; "Enron is certainly . . ." Yahoo! Chat, February 10, 2000; "Hell hath no fury . . ." *Business Week,* March 6, 2000.

DAMPIER: "For those investors . . ." BBC.com, April 18, 2000.

DENT: "Other Sources: *Contra Costa Times*, September 29, 2002; *New York Times*, *Time*, August 5, 2002; *San Antonio Express-News*, May 19, 2002.

DOBBS: "I have a great deal . . ." CNNfn, *Street Sweep*, October 2, 1997; "A program on corporate scandals . . ." *Austin American Statesman*, July 15, 2002; "SEC Chairman Arthur Levitt said . . ." CNN, *Moneyline*, April 13, 1999.

EBBERS: "Bernie was increasingly frustrated . . ." *Financial Times*, April 30, 2002; "WorldCom has a solid base . . ." Forbes.com, February 7, 2002. Other Sources: www.cbsnews.com, April 3, 2002; www.sanjosebizjournals.com, June 22, 2002; www.schwinger.harvard.edu.

ELIAS: "I think the market . . . "*Buffalo News*, September 26, 1999; "There's a high probability . . ." *Buffalo News*, April 5, 2000.

ERAIBA: "A classic investor reaction . . ." Cnet.com, July 26, 2000; "Well, actually . . ." CNNfn, *Ahead of the Curve*, October 5, 2000; "My sense: most of the decline . . ." CNNfn, *Market Coverage*, March 14, 2001; "Exceptionally strong . . ." CNNfn, *Market Coverage*, October 17, 2000. Other Source: *Crain Investment News*, November 20, 2000.

FARRELL: "We've got some rough sledding . . ." *St. Petersburg Times*, February 10, 2001; "step up to the plate . . ." *Nightly Business Report*, January 8, 2001; "I think the market . . ." CNN, *Moneyline*, June 3, 2002; "You mentioned the sell recommendations . . ." *Louis Rukeyser's Wall Street*, June 14, 2002; "I think we hit a bottom . . ." CNN *Moneyline*, June 6, 2002.

FLECKENSTEIN: "reckless" and "irresponsible" RealMoney.com, April 17, 2002; "yesterday's news" RealMoney.com, September 3, 2002; "the two-legged recipient . . ." RealMoney.com, September 12, 2002; "Un-American" CNN, *Moneyline*, July 27, 2001; "Volume of hate mail" RealMoney.com, November 11, 2002.

FOLKER: "We're a little more willing . . ." *Business Courier*, March 8, 2002; "undervalued" *Columbus Dispatch*, December 24, 2000; "buy on weakness" *Columbus Dispatch*, June 10, 2001; "mostly priced into the stocks" *Columbus Dispatch*, November 4, 2001.

GILDER: "still telling us . . ." and "If the judgment . . ." TheStreet.com, October 13, 2000. Other Source: *Chief Executive*, May 1999.

GLASSMAN: "most reliable route . . ." *Jewish World Review*, August 6, 2002.

GRAMM: "A long and difficult period . . . " *Consumer Bankruptcy News*, September 18, 2001; "bought Enron trading operation . . ." *New York Times*, October 22, 2002. Other Sources: *Oil Daily*, August 16, 2001; CNN, *Novak*,

Hunt & Shields, August 3, 2002; commoncause.org; Public Citizen; *Atlanta Journal and Constitution*, January 12, 2002.

GRASSO: "I want to send thank yous . . ." *Dallas Morning News*, March 30, 1999. Other Source: *Los Angeles Times*, January 1, 2000.

GREENSPAN: "I recognize . . ." *Wall Street Journal*, February 22, 2002. Other Sources: www.federalreserve.gov; www.dowjones.com; Federal Document Clearing House Political Transcripts, December 5, 2000.

GRIFFETH: "There are an awful lot . . ." ABC, *Nightline*, September 5, 2000; "I'm very confident . . ." CNBC, *Squawk Box*, June 22, 2001.

GRUBMAN: "The relentless series . . ." *Bloomberg News*, August 16, 2002; "I'm sculpting the industry . . ." *Business Week*, May 15, 2000; "The other word . . ." *Business Week*, May 15, 2000. Other Sources: AP, September 23, 2002; *New York Post*, August 30, 2002.

GUSTAFSON: "There really hasn't been . . ." CNN, *Lou Dobbs Moneyline*, July 2, 2001; "We're laying the groundwork . . ." *Bloomberg News*, June 18, 2002; "$4 billion . . ." CNN, *Lou Dobbs Moneyline*, December 13, 1999; "runs a $1.2 billion . . ." *Bloomberg News*, June 18, 2002.

HICKS: "I do this . . ." and "stupid" *Seattle Times*, December 17, 2000; "I'm not doing it . . ." www.espn.com, May 21, 2001; "I've never shot a mammal" *USA Today*, January 10, 2001. Other Source: www.dmagazine.com.

HOFFMAN: "I think we are going to . . ." CNBC, *Business Center*, December 31, 2001; "No matter what I think . . ." *Bloomberg News*, July 20, 2002. Other Source: www.talvest.com.

HOLLINGSWORTH: Other Sources: *Atlanta Business Chronicle*, July 27, 2001; *New York Times*, May 27, 2002.

HYMOWITZ: "dominating its space . . . Other Sources: CNNfn, *Market Coverage*, March 6, 2000. CNBC, *Business Center*, January 13, 2000; CNN, *Moneyline*, April 6, 2000, July 28, 2001; CNN, *Moneyweek*, December 18, 1999; CNBC, *Business Center*, September 17, 2002.

INSANA: "Let me ask you . . ." CNBC, *Business Center*, May 3, 2001; "Okay, you ready to go . . ." CNBC, *Business Center*, April 19, 2001.

JOSEPH: Other Sources: AFX—Asia, August 11, 2001; *Dallas Morning News*, August 3, 2001; *Adweek* Magazines' Technology Marketing, June 1, 2001; *South China Morning Post*, April 13, 2001.

JOSEPH COHEN: "In March 2000 I advised . . ." CNNfn, *September 11 Remembered*, September 11, 2002; "In March 2000, the day . . ." CNN, *Money Morning*, May 10, 2002; "I can assure you . . ." CNN, *Moneyline*, April 18,

2001. Other Sources: AP September 5, 2002; *USA Today*, May 29, 2000; *National Journal*, August 3, 2002.

KADLEC: "From where we stand . . ." *National Post*, November 29, 2001. Other Sources: www.census.gov; www.dowjones.com.

KANDEL: "I am sticking to my views . . ." CNN.com, December 31, 2000.

KARLGAARD: "the publishing, marketing . . ." *Wired*, July 2002; "There is no market . . ." *New York Times*, October 3, 2002.

KIGGEN: "ludicrously high . . ." *American Prospect*, February 12, 2001; "Using the fact . . ." *New York Times*, December 31, 2000; "should probably . . ." MarketWatch.com, November 27, 2002; "IPO profit sharing . . ." NASD press release, January 22, 2002. Other Sources: *American Prospect*, February 12, 2001; *Financial Times* (London), December 9, 2000; *New York Times*, September 15, 2002; TheStreet.com, February 15, 2000; *News and Observer* (Raleigh, North Carolina), March 10, 2000; *Contra Costa Times*, January 4, 2001.

KING: See Orman.

KOMANSKY: "Messrs. Komansky and O'Neal . . ." and "The [$100 million] settlement represents . . ." www.ML.com ; "I think the result . . ." *Nightly Business Report*, August 1, 2002. Other Source: *Guardian* (London), August 23, 2002.

KOZLOWSKI: Other Sources: Copley News Service, September 9, 2002; *New York Daily News*, August 15, 2002; *Slate*, September 12, 2002; *Independent* (London), September 12, 2002; *Calgary Herald*, September 28, 2002.

KUDLOW: "sizable stock market . . ." and "If you really want . . ." *National Review Online*, March 6, 2002; "For those of you . . ." *National Review* Online, July 15, 2002; "Could it be . . ." *National Review* Online, June 26, 2002; "but not for that . . ." CNBC, *Kudlow and Cramer*, August 23, 2002.

KURSON: "I definitely love money . . ." and "I don't appreciate irony" *New York Times*, July 26, 2001; "The key is to focus . . ." *Money*, June 10, 2002. Other Source: *Money*, June 10, 2002.

KUTTNER: "The 1920s and 1930s . . ." *Business Week*, March 20, 2000; "History will surely judge . . ." *New York Times*, December 17, 2000. Other Source: *Business Week*, February 5, 2001.

LAFFER: "Way undervalued . . ." CNBC, *Kudlow and Cramer*, September 13, 2002.

LAMBRO: "A clear and decisive . . ." *Washington Times*, November 29, 2001.

LAY: "I want to assure you . . ." *Washington Post*, January 13, 2002; "You're going to do what . . ." *Business Week* Online, August 24, 2001; "misleading" and "one-time" *Washington Post*, July 31, 2002; " 'one-time' loss derives from what the SEC describes as 'a series of complex hedging transactions' " www.sec.gov; "an outstanding job" and "a leave of absence" *Washington Post*, July 28, 2002. Other Sources: *Washington Post*, January 13, 2002; *Toronto Star*, August 25, 2002; *Daily Telegraph* (London), December 3, 2001.

LAYFIELD: "I told myself . . ." and "I've got all the chapters . . ." *Orlando* June 24, 2001. Other Sources: *National Post*, August 11, 2001; CNBC, *Squawk Box*, June 26, 2001.

LEVIN: "I want to put the poetry . . ." *Crain's New York Business*, December 10, 2001. Other Sources: *Daily Variety*, March 27, 2002; *New Yorker*, October 29, 2001.

LINDSEY: "You could've elected . . ." *Bloomberg News*, December 16, 2000; "Readers of this transcript . . ." FOMC Transcript, September 24, 1996. Other Source: *Washington Times*, January 17, 2002.

MCGINN: "For the foreseeable future . . ." RCR Wireless News, June 17, 2002. Other Sources: *Computer Reseller News*, June 24, 2002; *Contra Costa Times*, October 24, 2002; Radio Communications Report, November 1, 1999; *Tulsa World*, March 3, 2002.

MAYO: "was not . . ." Newhouse News Service; May 7, 2002, "anti-Blodget," *New York Observer*, November 26, 2001. Other Source: Congressional Testimony, June 14, 2001.

MEEKER: "offered biased research . . ." IndustryStandard.com, August 2, 2001; "She may be the greatest dealmaker . . ." and "I'm tired of the witch-hunt . . ." *Fortune*, May 21, 2001; "unavailable" IndustryStandard.com, June 5, 2001. Other Source: thestandard.com.

MESSIER: "For the first time . . ." *Times* (London), June 21, 2000. Other Sources: *Newsday*, April 30, 2002, June 20, 2000, July 2, 2002; *Times* (London), September 27, 2002; United Press International, September 13, 2002.

MONTY: "It's obvious that BCE . . ." CP, April 24, 2002. Other Sources: *National Post*, February 29, 2000; *Montreal Gazette*, May 30, 2002; *National Post*, April 25, 2002; *Broadcast News*, May 15, 2002.

MULLER: "Well, we do like companies . . ." *Motley Fool*, January 24, 2000.

NABI: "I cannot believe . . ." TheStreet.com, February 5, 2002; "The market is facing . . ." *Newsday*, June 4, 2002, "The shorts are playing . . ." *A.M.*, July 3, 2002.

NACCHIO: "Enronitis" CNNfn, *Moneyline*, February 14, 2002; "corporate McCarthyism" *Daily Deal*, March 11, 2002; "If these things . . ."

TheStreet.com, March 11, 2002; "After criss-crossing the globe . . ." *Times* (London), July 31, 2002. Other Sources: *Telephony*, December 17, 2001; *Wireless Week*, September 9, 2002; Science and Transportation Committee Hearing, July 30, 2002; Telco Business Report, September 23, 2002; *Newsbytes*, January 7, 2002.

NOTO: "buy" TheStreet.com, December 17, 1999; "survival" CNBC, *Business Center*, June 19, 2000; "The market sentiment . . ." CNN, *International E-Biz Asia*, December 30, 2000. Other Sources: *National Post*, January 9, 2001; *Los Angeles Business Journal*, March 5, 2001; *San Francisco Chronicle*, December 19, 2000.

ORLANDO: "Cheney would have had to know . . ." *Boston Globe*, June 2, 2002; "The two chief executives felt so comfortable . . ."*New York Times*, August 24, 2000; "like all major acquisitions . . ." and "easier and shorter" *Washington Post*, August 11, 2002. Other Sources: *Washington Post*, July 26, 2000; TheStreet.com, January 25, 1999; *Aberdeen Press and Journal*, May 21, 1999.

ORMAN: "You're in for the . . ." CNBC, *Business Center*, March 8, 2001. "This woman is never wrong!" CNN, *Larry King Live*, January 2, 2001; "Since the late 1990s . . ." CNBC, *The Suze Orman Show*, September, 2002. Other Source: www.dowjones.com.

PATERNOT: "The hottest initial public stock sale offering . . ." *Ottawa Citizen*, November 14, 1998; "the most euphoric moment . . ." and "You should always keep going . . ." CNN, M*overs with Jan Hopkins*, July 24, 1999. Other Sources: *San Antonio Express-News*, May 19, 2002; *Fortune*, September 16, 2002; *Herald* (Glasgow) August 8, 2001.

PIECYK: "Piecyk left Wall Street . . ." TheStreet.com, December 17, 2001; "Nokia already has strong market share . . ." *Electronic Buyers' News*, February 4, 2002. Other Sources: *Electronic Buyers' News*, June 12, 2000; *Telephony*, July 16, 2001.

PITT: Other Sources: *New York Daily News*, April 19, 2002; White House Bulletin, July 24, 2002; *New York Times*, July 24, 2002.

RAJAN: "I'm stunned . . ." CNNfn, *Street Life*, April 24, 2000; "I'm not sure . . ." BBC, *Wake Up to Money*, September 27, 2002. Other Source: CNNfn, *Market Coverage*, April 26, 2001.

REITZES: "The web is going to grow . . ." CNN, *Moneyweek*, January 22, 2000; "I think Cisco . . ." and "We've gone from a position . . ." CNN, *Moneyline Weekend*, February 3, 2001; "I've capitulated . . ." CNN, *Moneyweek*, March 17, 2001.

RIGAS: "looted Adelphia . . ." and "one of the most elaborate . . . frauds . . ." *Newsday*, July 25, 2002; "He has never sold a share . . ." Agence France-Presse, July 25, 2002. Other Sources: www.sec.gov; White House Bulletin, July 24, 2002; AP, July 16, 2002; *Seattle Post-Intelligencer*, July 24, 2002.

RILEY: "until the day I die" CNN, *Moneyline Weekend*, September 7, 2002.

ROTH: "Over the past twelve months . . ." *National Post*, November 1, 2001; "I will not be leaving . . ." *Montreal Gazette*, May 12, 2001; "A lot of people . . ." *National Post Business Magazine*, 2001. Other Sources: *National Post*, April 23, 2002; *New York Times*, June 16, 2001.

RUBIN: "Citicorp and Travelers Group expect . . ." www.citigroup.com. Other Sources: *NewsHour with Jim Lehrer*, July 1, 1999; *Washington Post*, October 27, 1999; Capitol Hill Hearings, June 17, 1998.

RUKEYSER: "I would remind folks . . ." NBC, *Today*, June 28, 2002.

RYNECKI: "The final years . . ." *Fortune*, June 11, 2001; "Call him the Insider" "But can Grubman cultivate . . ." and "dirt cheap" *Fortune*, December 18, 2000. Other Source: www.fortune.com.

SAEKI: "economic and market . . ." Nasdaq Japan press release, August 16, 2002; "Japan is more . . ." *Business Week*, March 19, 2001; Other sources: *Agence France Presse*, December 13, 2001; Nasdaq Japan press release, May 30, 2002.

SCHAFFLER: "You've pointed out . . ." and "you're still looking at . . ." CNNfn, *Market Call*, March 1, 2001.

SCHMID: Other Sources: *Financial Times* (London), May 7, 1997; *Irish Times*, September 28, 2002; *New York Times*, September 28, 2002; AP, September 25, 2002.

SCHREIBER: "We don't think . . ." *Los Angeles Times*, October 18, 2000; "uneducated institutional money . . ." *Boston Globe*, February 28, 2000; "Janus has been reducing . . ." *New York Times*, September 22, 2002. Other Source: CNBC, *Market Week with Maria Bartiromo*, December 29, 2001.

SCHUMER: "intensive and venal lobbying campaign" *New York Times*, January 19, 2002; "draconian" *Accounting Today*, July 10, 2000; "religion" CBS News, July 14, 2002; "One of the best things . . ." Federal News Service Press Conference, July 17, 2002; "It's our message . . ." CNBC, *News with Brian Williams*, July 23, 2002. Other Sources: Federal News Service, Capitol Hill Hearing, May 4, 2000; www.opensecrets.org.

SKILLING: "I am resigning . . ." Enron Press Release, PR Newswire, August 14, 2001. Other Sources: Cox News Service, March 21, 2002; www.enron.com.

SKRAINKA: "golden age . . ." and "this is going to impact . . ." *Los Angeles Times*, January 1, 2000; "The recession is over . . ." CNNfn, *Market Coverage*, April 8, 2002; "Well, in technology . . ." CNNfn, *Market Coverage*, March 7, 2000.

SMYTH: "We reiterate our view . . ." Agence France-Presse, March 12, 2001. Other Source: *Reno Gazette Journal*, July 14, 2002.

SONDERS: "Be careful in making investment decisions . . ." *Business Week* Online, November 29, 1999. Other Source: CNBC, *Louis Rukeyser's Wall Street*, May 3, 2002.

STEIN: "slight uptick in inflation" CNN, *NewsStand*, April 14, 2000; "was all taken away . . ." CNN, *NewsNight with Aaron Brown*, July 17, 2002; "Maybe the prices are ridiculous . . ." "Likely, this will all end . . ." and "Federal law prohibits gambling . . ." *Washington Post*, February 28, 1999. Other Source: www.benstein.com.

STEWART: "I just want to focus . . ." CBS, *Early Show*, June 25, 2002; "Stewart and other company insiders . . ." *San Francisco Chronicle*, August 23, 2002; "If she got hit . . ." *USA Today*, October 20, 1999. Other Sources: CNN, *Larry King Live*, February 2, 2000; *Christian Science Monitor*, August 27, 2002; *USA Today*, October 20, 1999; *Daily Mail* (London), September 13, 2002.

STREISAND: Other Sources: *USA Today*, August 13, 1999; *New York Observer*, August 23, 1999; *New York Post*, June 13, 1999.

SULLIVAN: "These are challenging times . . ." and "WorldCom is still the fastest-growing mega-cap . . ." *Business Week* Online, February 21, 2002; "I was instructed . . ." AP, September 27, 2002. Other Source: *CFO*, September, 1998.

THOMAN: "The plan called for . . ." AP, July 26, 2001. Other Source: *USA Today*, May 12, 2000; AP, April 15, 2000; *Detroit Free Press*, October 1, 2002.

TINDALL: Other Source: *New York Daily News*, February 16, 2001.

TURNER: "I am constantly amazed . . ." www.garth.ca, April 14, 2002.

WACHTEL: "I would not abandon . . ." CNNfn, *Market Coverage*, March 16, 2000; "Pray" *National Post*, June 1, 2002; I have made terrible . . ." *Houston Chronicle*, October 16, 2002. Other sources: *San Jose Mercury News*, December 30, 2000.

WAKSAL: "a train wreck" Hearing of the Oversight and Investigations Subcommittee of the House Energy and Commerce Committee, June 13, 2002. Other Sources: *Washington Post*, June 22, 2002; TheStreet.com, June 13, 2002.

PRINCE AL-WALEED: "I'm the Al Waleed . . ." and "So please . . ." CNBC, *Business Center,* May 16, 2001. Other Sources: CNN, *Moneyline,* November 15, 2000, and November 16, 2000.

WANG: "I think the vote speaks . . ." *Newsday,* August 26, 1999. Other Sources: *Austin American-Statesman,* October 11, 1999; *Financial Times* (London), August 31, 1999; *Business Week,* August 30, 2002.

WARD: "I'm clearly an NBA player . . ." *U.S. News & World Report,* May 21, 2001; "I always had this vision . . ." www.ABCnews.com.

WEILL: "Mr. Weill never told . . ." AP, August 23, 2002; "a fresh look . . ." Business Wire, November 12, 2002. Other Sources: *National Post,* April 7, 1998; CNNfn, *Market Coverage,* April 6, 1999; *New York Times,* December 20, 2002; Slate.com, November 15, 2002.

WEINGARTEN: "the majority of money managers . . ." *Sunday Herald Sun* (Melbourne), September 15, 2002; "as you may know . . ." and "Anybody who doesn't see . . ." *National Journal,* August 3, 2002.

WHITE: "We effectively are the CEOs . . ." Department of Defense Briefing, June 18, 2001; "I am responsible . . ." and "I took straight . . ." Science and Transportation Committee, July 18, 2002. Other Sources: www.enron.com, www.whitehouse.gov.

WILLIAMS: "Dear Larry . . ." and "Ebbers is the man . . ." www.upside.com.

WINCH: "an accounting fraud . . ." SEC press release, January 13, 1999. Other Sources: *Los Angeles Times,* July 1, 1989; *Chicago Sun-Times,* August 13, 1998; *Bloomberg News,* September 11, 1999; www.sec.gov; CNNfn, *Before Hours,* April 15, 1998.

WINNICK: "The only legacy . . ." Cnet.com, October 2, 2002; "I know I can go back . . ." *Contra Costa Times,* October 13, 2000. Other Sources: AP Online, August 10, 2002; *New York Daily News,* August 10, 2002; Cox News Service, April 21, 2002; PR Newswire, August 14, 1998; *Bloomberg News,* September 28, 1999; *New York Times,* May 18, 1999; *Jewish Journal,* October 1, 1999; *Fortune,* June 24, 2002; *Time,* June 17, 2002; *New York Times,* July 14, 2002.